THE CONSTELLATIONS

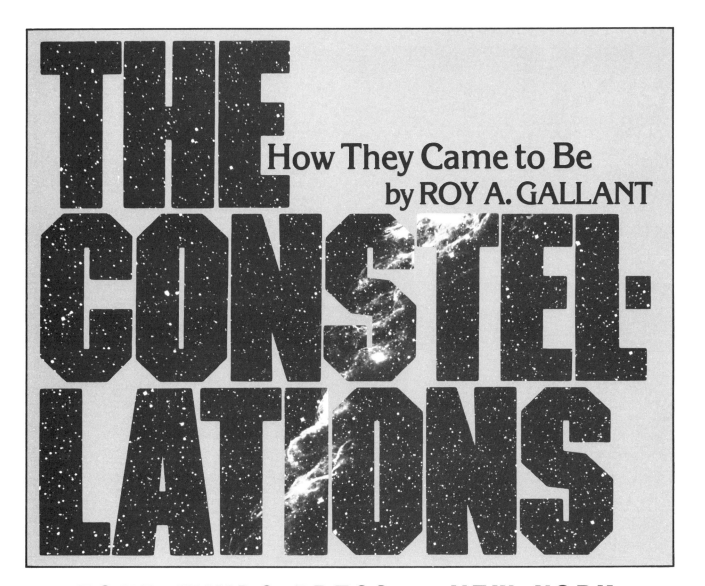

THE CONSTEL-LATIONS

How They Came to Be
by ROY A. GALLANT

FOUR WINDS PRESS * NEW YORK

Revised edition 1991
Four Winds Press
Macmillan Publishing Company
866 Third Avenue
New York, NY 10022
Collier Macmillan Canada, Inc.
1200 Eglinton Avenue East
Suite 200
Don Mills, Ontario M3C 3N1
Printed and bound in the United States of America
Book design by Constance Ftera
Drawings by Constance Ftera

10 9 8 7 6 5 4 3 2 1

Library of Congress Cataloging-in-Publication Data
Gallant, Roy A.
    The constellations, how they came to be.
    Includes index.
    SUMMARY: A guide to identifying constellations
with an explanation of the mythology surrounding them.
    1. Constellations—Juvenile literature. [1. Con-
stellations. 2. Mythology] I. Title.
QB802.G26   398.2'6   79-12816
ISBN 0-02-735776-7

For Fred

Capricornus   Aquarius   Pisces   Aries   Thaurus

On this great drawing board of the night, diagrams
have been scrawled in mathematical reverie. But
they are false. All these constellations are beautifully false. For stars, which are, in fact, completely
separate, are joined in a single figure. Imaginary
lines are drawn between the points of reality,
where isolated stars gleam like diamonds. The
dream, like a great master of abstract painting, has
used a bare minimum of points to portray all the
animals of the Zodiac . . . that Rorschach Test of
all humanity.

—GASTON BACHELARD

Gemini   Cancer   Leo   Uirgo   Libra

These engravings of the twelve signs of the Zodiac were made by Bernhard Maler and appeared in Hyginus's *Poeticon Astronomicon,* dated 1482.

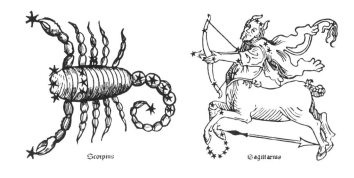

Scorpius　　　　Sagittarius

Acknowledgments

I wish to thank Doubleday & Company, Inc., for letting me use four brief excerpts from my book *Astrology: Sense or Nonsense?* Copyright 1974 by Roy A. Gallant. I also wish to thank my present publisher, Four Winds Press, for letting me use brief excerpts from my book *Fires in the Sky: The Birth and Death of Stars* Copyright 1978 by Roy A. Gallant.

The Blackfoot star legends retold in this book are based on material appearing in a small publication entitled *Star Legends Among the American Indians* (Science Guide 91) by Clark Wissler, Late Curator Emeritus of Anthropology, The American Museum of Natural History, New York, New York.

My special thanks to Dr. Mark R. Chartrand III, former Chairman, The American Museum-Hayden Planetarium, for his many valuable suggestions for this book when it was in the outline stage, and for his careful reading of the completed manuscript. My thanks also to Gloria Gutwirth for reviewing the Greek and Roman mythological and historical material. And finally my thanks to the Richard S. Perkin Library of The American Museum-Hayden Planetarium for its excellent resources and helpful personnel.

Contents

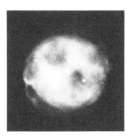

Introduction

Think back a bit: Maybe you remember when the Voyager spacecraft were sent on their historic journeys to the outer planets, when you first heard of black holes, pulsars, quasars, or the rings of Uranus.

These are only a few of many developments that have taken place in astronomy over the past few decades: new kinds of objects, new cosmic frontiers, new and deeper understanding of how stars form, live, and die. Our knowledge of the Universe is incomparably greater and richer than that of the Greeks, the Egyptians, or, before them, the Sumerians.

But the sky remains the same!

The sky you can see on any clear, dark night differs little from that seen by those first astronomer-priests, those nomadic shepherds of the Fertile Crescent, or the astrologers of the ancient courts of China. Even so, a casual look into the night sky strikes awe into most people today. It has been so since the time, indescribably long ago, that the first person looked upward.

The constellations, myths, legends, stories, and superstitions about the sky are the result and legacy of that awe. With every change in our view of the Universe have come changes in our view of ourselves —the legends of ancient civilizations are reflections of their world-pictures. They give us a way of looking into what they knew and thought.

But, aside from this, what good are the constellations and a knowledge of them and their stories? Well . . . what good is it to know the names of the trees and birds on a walk through the woods, or those of the fish for a dive on a coral reef? They are all part of nature, as are we. A knowledge of the sky can make you feel at home under the stars, can provide you with an unerring compass and clock and calendar, and link you to peoples who studied the stars long, long ago. And, if simply knowing your way around the sky makes you want to know more of the details of the universe, so much the better.

These are the functions of this book. Whether you share the crackling winter nights of the author, or the warmer nights farther south, the sky is pretty much the same for all of us in the temperate regions of the Northern Hemisphere. This book is designed to help you enjoy the night sky.

After a few clear nights of making the acquaintance of the constellations, don't be surprised if, ever afterwards, your first impulse upon going out of doors is to look up!

Dr. Mark R. Chartrand III
Former Chairman
The American Museum-Hayden Planetarium

THE CONSTELLATIONS

A Preview

The sky is an evening's entertainment. It is free and there for the viewing on any clear night. The night sky is alive with meteors, the planets creeping slowly among the stars, and a vast gallery of imaginary figures—the constellations. And once in a while you may expect to see a comet, not to mention a host of artificial satellites racing this way and that among the background stars.

Once you know some of the many myths associated with the stars and constellations, the night sky becomes a splendid picture book brimming with adventures of mythical heroes, maidens, and monsters. With just a little practice you will soon learn to find your way among the more than forty constellation figures described in this book, and before very long you will begin to feel very much at home with them.

On a clear night, from either the Northern or Southern Hemisphere you can see about 1,500 stars with the unaided eye. These stars range from first magnitude through sixth magnitude. (See Glossary for an explanation of "magnitude.") A pair of 7-

The Magnitude of Stars

1st	2nd	3rd	4th	5th	6th	
10	35	110	250	345	750	= 1,500 TOTAL

power binoculars will reveal a few thousand more stars than you can see with the unaided eye. A 3-inch telescope will bring into view about half a million. Among the objects you can expect to see with binoculars are variable stars, double stars, and several galaxies far beyond our own. But you will also see many of these same objects with your eyes alone. These can be thrilling sights to the amateur astronomer seriously looking at the night sky for the first time. Let the pages ahead guide you through the night sky season by season. As you observe, you will find yourself asking many questions and wondering what this or that object is, how far away it is, what it is made of, and what is happening to it. Many of the answers are bound to surprise you.

The constellations—Orion the Hunter, Leo the Lion, Taurus the Bull, and nearly 100 others—were invented by ancient people long before the science of astronomy was born. These people looked on the stars as objects having a life force, as objects that could bring good fortune beyond one's wildest dreams. How the constellations and stars came to be looked on in this way is the subject of this book.

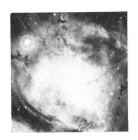

Patterns in the Sky

If we want to understand how and why the constellations came to be invented, and how they were used, we have to turn the clock back many thousands of years. We must return to a time when people looked on the night sky as a source of fear and comfort, of hope and despair, but most of all as a place of wonder and mystery. The sky also was a vast battlefield where gods and demons fought in deadly combat and from which they controlled the ways of man.

The sky was the calendar of ancient peoples. By remembering year after year that a certain star, or certain groups of stars, rose with the Sun at dawn, or disappeared in the darkening sky just after sunset, they could predict the coming of spring, winter, and the other seasons.

We can be certain that ancient people looked on the blackboard sky, and the many events nightly chalked there, with wonder and mystery. Our evidence is the tapestry of fanciful stories about the stars, dating back at least 5,000 years ago, that have

In days of old, optical illusions caused by atmospheric conditions, such as mock Suns, or "Sun dogs," were frightening. This woodcut, done in 1563 shows such "parhelic phenomena." COURTESY OF THE ZENTRAL BIBLIOTHEK, ZURICH.

been handed down to us. Those dusty records tell us that ancient peoples the world over based their religions on the astronomical events they saw occurring in the sky. The invention of gods, demons, and an endless train of myths relating them to the stars was not done simply for amusement. It was done in deadly earnest.

The invention of these elaborate creatures of the night painted on the sky served very useful purposes. One was an early attempt to explain the many motions of a bewildering number and variety of sky objects—Sun, Moon, planets, stars, comets, and meteors—as well as such puzzling occurrences as lightning, rain, and auroras. At the time we are talking about, people did not understand the real difference between stars and planets. They did not know what comets and meteors were or what caused the night sky sometimes to glow as an aurora.

Without a scientific approach to guide them in their search for knowledge, these people relied on a far easier way of explaining what they observed. That way was superstition, a blindly accepted belief that *seems* to answer a question. For instance, early Chinese astronomers believed that the first yearly appearance of the star Arcturus was the *cause* of spring. And the ancient Egyptians believed that the yearly flooding of the River Nile was *caused* by the "power" of the star Sirius. By studying the old myths about the stars and constellations, we can learn much about the ways people of old viewed the world. Many of those beliefs have been handed down through time and form the basis of many things we ourselves believe today. A large number of the very words and expressions we use today have their roots in star-words used by the old stargazers; for example, "you can bet your lucky stars." Our words *influence*, *influenza*, and *influx* all come from the Latin word *influentia*, which means "emanation of ethereal fluid from the heavens affecting mankind." *Disaster* means "evil star." The word *consider* comes from *considare*, which means "to observe stars carefully for an omen." The word *desire* comes from *desidere*, meaning "without a star," and "the outcome unfulfilled."

Because the stars were unknowable as physical

objects to people of ancient times, they provided an excellent way of fulfilling the eternal and universal wish for a life after death. People do not like sad endings, and those mysterious objects, the stars, seemed to provide a happy ending to their spent lives by being the places where they could continue their lives after death. In the year 421 B.C., a comic play entitled *Peace*, by the Greek writer Aristophanes, assured its audience that servants, as well as their masters and national heroes, might look forward to stardom. In one light moment one of the characters in the play asks who the shooting stars are. He is told that "they are people bearing torches and just returning from a dinner party given by one of the richer stars."

At least a thousand years before Aristophanes' time, the Egyptians were writing accounts of the dead being "reborn" as stars. The Egyptian hiero-

It takes much imagination and invention to see in any star group the amount of detail shown in this old representation of Orion, the Hunter.

glyph from which we get our star-sign ✳ means "soul."

The ancient Chinese looked on the stars as souls waiting to be born. In the ancient Chinese *Annals of the Bamboo Books* are accounts of the birth of a line of emperors. All began as detached souls in the form of fiery light. Then as shooting stars, one by one, they entered a human embryo being carried by the various mothers of these emperors-to-be. The emperors thus born, according to the accounts, entered this world at various times from 2689 B.C. to 2205 B.C.

Such notions seem farfetched to us today but they have been quite real to people throughout history and until only a few centuries ago. The

Just before dark the lights of a village appear as shown in this sketch. The more distant a street light, the fainter it appears to the eye (top). Below is how our village-constellation appears when darkness falls. This is how the various stars forming a given constellation actually are arranged in space—some nearer, others farther away. COURTESY: LAROUSSE ASTRONOMY.

world was seen as a blend of reality and fantasy. That part of the mind that invents myths and gives shape to the fearsome make-believe creatures that haunt us played a major role in the lives of people who lived before writing was invented. And to this day it continues to play an important role in the lives of children, and of most adults as well.

Another important purpose that these fanciful stories about the sky served was a way of remembering the positions of the stars and planets. If the mind's eye could imagine a group of stars in the shape of a bear or whale, for example, remembering what part of the sky such an animal tramped over or swam through from night to night would be easier than trying to remember the changing pattern of an unrelated group of stars. The first star and constellation myths must have been spun long, long before writing had been invented and were handed down from one generation to the next by storytellers. So it seems likely that the very ancient stargazers had no way of keeping written records of what went on in the sky; they had only their memories to rely on. Again, it is much easier to remember events or objects if we associate them with pictures, so why not invent stories about such events and so make a kind of private motion picture of them, a picture easily remembered by the mind's eye.

ENTER THE SUMERIANS☆☆☆☆☆☆☆☆☆☆☆☆☆☆☆☆☆☆☆
It is in this kind of climate of thinking that we must put ourselves if we are to see the world through the eyes of the old mythmakers. Around 5000 B.C., a people known as Sumerians were settled in the Middle East between the eastern end of the Mediterranean Sea and the Persian Gulf. Here lay *The Arabian Nights* fable lands of twelve centuries ago, the Garden of Eden, the Hanging Gardens of Babylon, and the home of Abraham.

The Sumerians were not a primitive people. They were skilled farmers, and they had a calendar and a highly developed system of writing, the first writing we know of. The written records left on clay tablets by the Sumerians tell us that they looked

Many clay tablets like this one made by the Sumerians and dated around 3500 B.C. consist of records of astronomical observations, showing that astronomy as a science is at least 5,500 years old.

down on nomadic groups as "people who do not know houses and who do not cultivate wheat." When men learned to work the land, and settled in large communities, they had a need to write. They became property owners and traders of goods. Records had to be kept, taxes had to be computed, and the laws of the community had to be written down for all to see. And, just as important, from a religious point of view, the astronomer-priests needed a way to keep day-to-day, month-to-month, and year-to-year records of the changing positions of the Sun, Moon, and stars. Such records became a calendar which enabled these wizards of old to foretell the arrival of the seasons. This knowledge was extremely valuable to early agricultural communities.

The Sumerians believed in a supergod who ruled over a number of lesser gods. The supergod was called Anu, a word meaning "that which is above." Eclipses were then looked on as times of great danger, and it was the role of the astronomer-priests to protect the land and its people. The Moon, Sun, and other sky objects regarded as gods were imagined to have personal feelings and so had to be consoled in times of stress. Sacrifices had to be made to comfort and appease them. During an eclipse of the Moon, Sin, the Moon-god, was thought to be attacked by demons and to be in great pain. This is what accounted for the Moon's growing dimmer and dimmer during the first part of the eclipse. As soon as an eclipse began to take place, the priests, according to ritual, had to light a torch on the temple altar and recite chants to save the fields, rivers, and other parts of the land from destruction. Meanwhile, all the people had to cover their heads with their clothing and shout loudly, which always seemed to help restore things to normal. Who could deny that such ritual worked? Obviously it did, since the eclipse passed and the land was not harmed. So great was the people's fear of unusual events in the sky that few would have been likely to have had the courage to do nothing at all in order to find out just what would or would not happen.

Over many generations the Sumerians and then the Babylonians, who later conquered them, recorded the patterns of motions of those sky objects visible to them. The Sun and Moon were the two most conspicuous objects, the Sun being the more "important" of the two. After all, the Sun governed the behavior and well-being of all living things and brought night and day. As "giver of life," the Sun was regarded by ancient peoples as the source of the stars as well. The Sun was thought to be born anew each day. Then in the evening when it set, the Sun was thought to burst into tiny pieces, its fragments scattering far and wide and becoming the stars that soon appeared.

MOTIONS IN THE SKY ☆☆☆☆☆☆☆☆☆☆☆☆☆☆☆☆☆☆☆

The early stargazers did not have to be astrophysicists to figure out the daily, monthly and yearly motion patterns of the Moon and Sun. Today we can show that the Sun is located at the center of the Solar System and that Earth and all the other planets revolve about the Sun. But it took nearly 5,000 years for this view of the Solar System to be accepted. Until the 1500s, people generally supposed that Earth stood motionless and that the Sun, Moon, planets, and stars all revolved about Earth. They also thought that Earth occupied the central point in the Universe. And that was just what their senses told them. After all, they could not *feel* Earth move as it rotated on its axis or as it revolved about the Sun. And wasn't the Sun seen to rise over the same horizon each morning and set below the opposite horizon each evening? And wasn't the Moon seen to rise and then move across the great sky dome and set over the opposite horizon in much the same way? And what of the stars? They, too, were seen to parade across the night sky as a group, never seeming to change position relative to one another. That is why they came to be called the "fixed" stars. Some "stars," however, were not fixed but seemed to wander back and forth among the background stars. These were the planets.

The stargazers of old firmly believed that there was a strong relationship among the stars and planets, the gods, the weather, earthquakes, and all other natural events. Downpours supposedly were caused when a leak occurred in the great sky dome —called the "firmament"—and so let a heavenly ocean of water cascade through. We will meet this great ocean of the sky, and the monsters inhabiting it, several times later on when we take up the constellations. In *Genesis*, the biblical flood is accounted for in this way: ". . . the windows of heaven were opened. And the rain was upon the Earth forty days and forty nights." Observing that rainy seasons occurred in patterns—the monsoons, for example—the astronomer-priests of old supposed that the position of the Sun as it entered and passed through various constellations was the cause. For that reason they invented three "watery" constellations in that section of the sky where the Sun was located during the rainy season. Those constellations are Pisces, the Fishes, Aquarius, the Water-Carrier, and Capricornus, the Sea-Goat. Another watery constellation sharing that same section of sky is Cetus, the Whale.

Believing in a relationship between the heavenly bodies and earthly events, the ancients reasoned that if they could learn more about the motions of the Sun, Moon, and stars, they would be in a better position to predict the weather, the onset of the changing seasons, and other natural events. They also believed that they would be better able to serve those gods of the sky and in so doing improve mankind's lot on Earth.

THE MOON'S APPARENT MOTION ☆☆☆☆☆☆☆

The Moon's apparent motion against the background of fixed stars was the easiest to work out. Each night the Moon could be seen to rise in the east and arc its way across the great sky dome, or *celestial sphere*, toward the west. As it did, it could be seen repeatedly to follow a fixed course through the same train of constellations month after month. It also was a simple matter for the early stargazers to count the number of days it took the Moon to go through one complete phase change from full moon to new moon and back to full moon again. The time taken was a little less than 30 days.

THE SUN'S APPARENT MOTION ☆☆☆☆☆☆☆☆☆☆

The Sun's course across the sky dome was a bit harder to trace, since the stars were invisible by day. Even so, it could be traced accurately. Moments before sunrise, just before the stars fade from view, you can see part of a constellation behind the Sun. The particular constellation you see, of course, depends on the time of the year you are looking. At sunset, in the same way, you can see part of a different constellation forming the background of stars on the celestial sphere. Again, the particular constellation you happen to see will depend on what time of the year you are looking. During the day, of course, we cannot see the stars (although once in a while we can see a particularly bright one if we know just where to look), so we cannot see the Sun's path against the background of stars.

There are times, however, when we can see the

stars very clearly during the day. During a total eclipse of the Sun, when the Moon blocks out the Sun, the stars gradually appear as more and more of the Sun's disk is hidden and the sky grows darker. During such times the Sun's position against the background constellations can be seen. But again, we don't have to see those stars in order to know the Sun's path across their background.

By the time the Greek astronomers seriously turned their attention to the stars (around 500 B.C.), they had enough records of observations made by the Babylonians to chart the Sun's course across the celestial sphere without even observing the Sun at dawn and dusk. Their resulting view, or *model*, as scientists say, of the celestial sphere showed very accurately just what constellations happened to be behind the Sun or behind the Moon at any moment of day or night. The point is that once the Greeks had accumulated enough

This representation of the Zodiac belt of twelve constellations is from *Textus de sphaera*, published in 1531.

records of past observations—their own and those of the Babylonians—they no longer had to go outside and look to find out where the Moon was in relation to a given constellation. Their tables told them, just as do the astronomical tables used by astronomers today.

What about those "wandering stars," the planets? What paths did they trace across the celestial sphere? That, too, was easy enough for the ancient stargazers to figure out. During the nighttime, the paths followed by Mars, Jupiter, and Saturn across the constellations could be easily seen; and the paths followed by the remaining two planets recognized at the time—Mercury and Venus—also were known since those two planets followed along with the Sun. It turned out that the Sun, Moon, and five known planets all moved along the same path across the surface of the celestial sphere. All passed through, one after another, with each constellation forming that celestial highway that came to be called the *Zodiac*. The "center line" along that highway traveled by the Sun,

Moon, and planets is called the *ecliptic*. We will return to the Zodiac and ecliptic later.

CAUSE OF THE SEASONS ☆☆☆☆☆☆☆☆☆☆☆☆☆☆☆☆

The ancients were interested in another pattern of motion of the Sun, one that was very important to them in carrying out their farming activities. As the Sun was seen to climb higher and higher in the sky day by day, it signaled the coming of spring and the warm weather and rains needed for the successful planting and growth of crops.

Most people are aware that as winter gives way to spring, and spring to summer, each day the noon Sun climbs a bit higher in the sky than on previous days. And because of the Sun's new and higher position, each day grows a little warmer. It is warmer because the Sun's rays are striking us from more directly overhead than before. Then as summer gives way to fall, and fall to winter, each day the noon Sun appears a bit lower in the sky and each day the air grows a little cooler.

In the Northern Hemisphere summer begins on

June 22 (see diagram), at which time the noon Sun appears at its highest point in the sky. That marks the official beginning of summer and is the day when we in the Northern Hemisphere have the greatest number of daylight hours. This is the time called *Summer Solstice*. After that the days become shorter and the nights longer, until, at official autumn, about September 21, the hours of day and night are equal. This time is called *Autumnal Equinox*.

Although the ancients could not know it, Earth is tilted a bit in relation to its orbit. Because it is tilted, and remains so as it circles the Sun, the Northern Hemisphere is tilted away from the Sun for three months after Autumnal Equinox. By about December 22, the noon Sun is low in the sky as seen from the Northern Hemisphere. So the Northern Hemisphere now receives the Sun's rays at a low angle, which means the least amount of heating. This first day of winter marks the shortest day of the year and is called *Winter Solstice*, at which time the Sun begins its apparent motion

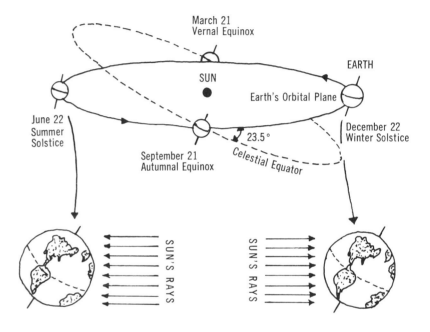

The seasons are caused by Earth's obliquity, or the amount by which it is tilted in space. As a result of its obliquity, a given location on Earth's surface receives varying amounts of insulation at different times of the year. See text for details.

northward. The Southern Hemisphere now receives the high direct rays of the Sun and enjoys long summer days. Three months later, about March 21, the length of day and night again are equal, marking the arrival of spring, called *Vernal Equinox*. Each day from now on, the days gradually grow warmer.

This up-and-down motion across the sky of the noon Sun throughout the year was known by the Egyptian astronomer-priests at least 5,000 years ago. It was used by them to regulate the farming activities on which the well-being of their kingdom depended. We will see many instances of this later on when we consider the constellations.

So important was the role played by the Sun in the lives of farming cultures the world over in pre-historic times that religions based on a Sun-god were common. Without an understanding of the chemistry of the soil and how heat influences plant growth, it is understandable why early peoples thought of the Sun as a god, a bringer of life. Since the Sun gives life to the plant world each year, then why not suppose that in the beginning it also gave

life to man? In short, why not regard it as the "god of creation"? Many early peoples did.

A ZUÑI CREATION LEGEND ☆☆☆☆☆☆☆☆☆☆☆☆

Among those peoples who looked on the Sun as a god are New Mexico's Zuñi Indians. According to Zuñi creation legends, originally there were no people on Earth's surface. They were all crowded into a large dark dungeon four levels underground. The Sun-god felt sorry for the imprisoned people, so he called his two sons to his side and said, "Let the people into the light." The two sons went down to Earth and entered the four lower worlds. Each world became darker and darker. When the sons finally reached the people they said, "We have come for you."

"Bring us to the Sun," the people cried.

As they followed the two boys, the people's eyes hurt as they climbed up to the lighter third world and the even lighter second world. "Is this the bright world where we are to live?" the people asked. "Not yet," answered the two boys.

When the people stepped out into the fresh air and bright light they were blinded. The Sun's rays pained them so that tears streamed from their eyes. And as their tears mixed with the soil, buttercups and sunflowers began to grow.

"This is the world," the people said.

A BLACKFOOT LEGEND☆☆☆☆☆☆☆☆☆☆☆☆☆☆☆☆

There are many Blackfoot Indian myths explaining the puzzling picture of the night sky. One such myth tells us how the Sun and Moon came to be. The myth was recorded by Clark Wissler, Late Curator Emeritus of Anthropology, The American Museum of Natural History. It was told to him by Wolf-head, a Blackfoot Indian who said that he was born sometime around the year 1850. The myth is as follows:

The Sun was a brother and the Moon the sister in a family of long ago, according to Wolf-head. Often they quarreled. Upon one occasion the sister was so outraged over the treatment she received at the hands of her brother that she grasped a burning stick from the house fire and rushed up through the smoke hole of the tipi. The brother, shouting that she could not escape him in that way, caught up a larger firebrand and followed in pursuit. So they continue to this day, the Moon with the fainter light moving across the sky at night, the Sun with his great firebrand still pursuing the Moon and causing the day.

The theme of this myth is not restricted to the Blackfoot Indians, Wissler tells us, but was spread among Indian tribes ranging from Cape Cod to Alaska. Stranger even than the myth itself is how such a myth becomes popular and ingrained in the thinking of peoples living very far away from each other.

A SUMA LEGEND ☆☆☆☆☆☆☆☆☆☆☆☆☆☆☆☆☆☆☆☆

The Suma Indians of Central America also have a creation myth accounting for the way life arose on Earth. In the beginning, it goes, there were two brothers, the older one named Papan (which in the Suma language means father). They wandered about Earth. They made the forests and grasslands, dug rivers, and created the hills. During a canoe trip, as they were trying to decide what they should create next, they capsized and were forced to swim to shore. To dry and warm themselves they built a fire. A bird flying high overhead caught Papan's eye. As he watched it gliding gracefully on the wind, he backed into the fire, burst into flames, and was carried high into the heavens. He became the Sun. The Suma myth says that Papan's rays created the Suma people. And they refer to him as Ma-Papan, which in Suma language means Sun-father. The younger brother also stepped into the fire and was carried into the sky. But he put up such a struggle that sparks flew across the heavens. He became the Moon, and his sparks became the stars.

There are other such stories that cast the Sun in the role of creator of mankind and all life on Earth. In Egyptian mythology, life was created by the god Atum. At first, according to the story, there was only vast ocean called Nun covering Earth. Then Atum, which means "everything" and "nothing,"

created himself. He arose from the sea and created a small mound of earth to stand on. In old Egyptian writing the sign for this mound is ☀. It means to "shine forth." When Atum became the ruler of creation, his name was changed to Atum-Ra (*Ra* means "Sun").

There are other Egyptian creation myths which vary slightly from the Atum-Ra story. One has Amon (the wind) and Ra (the Sun) as a single force—Amon-Ra—giving life to Earth. Another has Khnum, which possibly means "animals' ability to reproduce," joining forces with Ra to become Khnum-Ra. In any case, the observed power of the Sun to bring life to the land may have been behind the Egyptians' naming their creator-gods Ra.

Other peoples of the world must also have read into the Sun the same power to create life. The Yahao Chins of Burma thought that the Sun laid an egg from which they were hatched. And the Incas of Peru looked on the Sun as creator of the Incas and the world. The Yuchi Indians of eastern Tennessee called themselves "People of the Sun."

Invent
Your Own
Constellations

The fact that ancient people, like people today, regarded the world as a blend of fact and fancy is nowhere better shown than in the countless myths that have been painted on the great sky dome. The drawings on the next page show how the mind's eye can visualize different shapes out of a grouping of points.

The five dots represent stars in the constellation Boötes, about which we will have more to say later (see page 151). Notice that we can link these stars with lines in at least three ways (1, 2, 3). When we do we end up with three quite different geometric shapes. If we use our imagination we can translate those geometric shapes into objects familiar to us. In this way we can create our own private constellations, the Kite (4), the Pointed Ghost (5), the Broken Jug (6), or the Pitcher (7).

Why not try your hand at linking the stars of each constellation in your own way, first to form a simple geometric shape, and then using your imagination to create a recognizable animal or other figure. This is an excellent way of remembering the constellations and the various stars they contain. If you work at it gradually you will end up with your own sky theater inhabited with figures of your own invention. You can even make up stories about each figure, and about certain clusters of two or more constellations that lie near each other. One example of such a grouping of constellations is Andromeda, Cassiopeia, Perseus, Cepheus, and Cetus, which you will read about in the next section.

BOÖTES

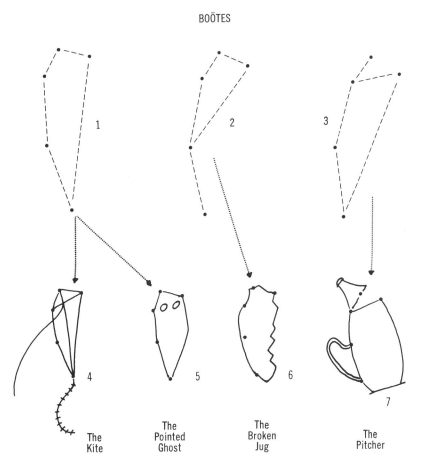

1

2

3

4
The Kite

5
The Pointed Ghost

6
The Broken Jug

7
The Pitcher

Create your own constellations. Shown here are five of the main stars of the constellation Boötes. Notice that the relative positions of the five stars in Figures 1, 2, and 3 have not been changed but that the dots in each figure have been linked to form different geometric shapes. Then each of those three geometric shapes, with a little imagination, can be elaborated into familiar objects of your choice.

The North Polar Sky

Since there is no "proper" place in the sky to begin a survey of the constellations, we can begin anywhere we like. So let's begin with those stars grouped around and near the north polar sky and find what stories they have to tell. Astronomers call this grouping of stars the *north circumpolar stars*.

First of all what can you expect to see when you look at this part of the sky? The center of the map, and the point just about right overhead in the sky as seen from the North Pole, is marked by the North Star, called Polaris. This star marks the tail-end of the Little Dipper, or Ursa Minor, meaning the "Lesser Bear." The Big Dipper, which is the easiest star group in the sky to find, points the way to Polaris. Just follow the two stars forming the end of the dipper, opposite the handle-end, Merak and Dubhe, and they point right to Polaris. That is why they are called "the Pointers."

The middle star of the three making up the Big Dipper's handle, Mizar, is a double star. If you look at Mizar just the right way you will see a faint

21

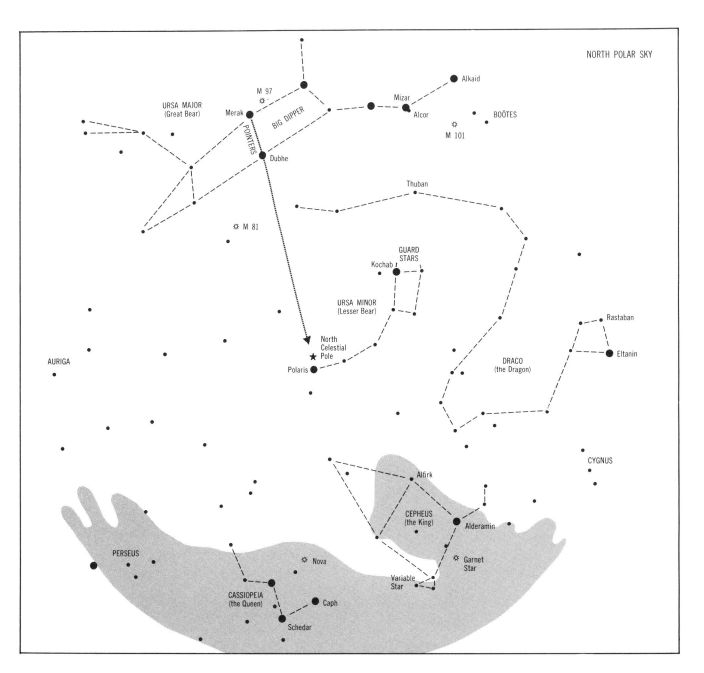

companion-star, Alcor. The Big Dipper, by the way, is not a constellation. It is a group of stars forming part of the constellation known as Ursa Major, or the Great Bear.

In addition to the two dippers, you will find Draco, the Dragon, in the north polar sky. Draco winds his way across the sky in a great "S," his tail separating the two dippers. The star Eltanin marked in Draco's head is also a double star, but you will need binoculars to split this seemingly single star into two separate ones.

Cepheus, the King, also belongs to this part of the northern sky, as does his wife, Queen Cassiopeia. The star Alfirk marked in Cepheus is also a double star. But again, you will need binoculars to split it

The north circumpolar star chart shows only those constellation figures mentioned in the text, although numerous additional stars are shown. The large-dot stars represent stars of magnitude 2 to 2.5. The small-dot stars represent stars of magnitude less than 2.5. The light shaded area represents the Milky Way.

into a white star with a dimmer blue companion. The yellow star of this pair is a variable star. If you watch it nightly, you will find that it gradually grows brighter, then gradually becomes dimmer, and then grows brighter again. It completes one cycle from bright to dim and back to bright again in about five days. To find out more about variable stars, see the GLOSSARY, page 195.

Cassiopeia lies almost directly across the sky from the Big Dipper and right beside her husband, Cepheus. Binoculars will show several interesting objects in and around Cassiopeia's field of five stars, which form an "M" or "W." You may expect to see double stars and a number of star clusters. If you have a telescope, you should be able to see a magnificent spiral galaxy, known as M 81, near Dubhe, the top pointer-star in the Big Dipper. M 97, the Owl Nebula, also can be seen near the Big Dipper beside Merak, the other pointer-star. A word of warning here is in order. Although the photographs of various sky objects in this book show the objects as splendid sights, don't expect binoculars to reveal them to you in this way. Most will appear as tiny fuzzy patches. Even so, the photographs will help you see certain details that you would be unaware of without the help of the photographs.

POLARIS (the North Star) ☆☆☆☆☆☆☆☆☆☆☆☆☆☆☆☆☆☆☆☆

Perhaps more than any star other than the Sun, Polaris has been regarded as the most important star in the heavens. Located almost directly overhead as seen from the North Pole, it is the end-star in the tail of Ursa Minor, the Little Bear. Its name comes to us from the Latin, *Stella Polaris*, meaning "Pole Star." Polaris has long been an important star to sailors, caravans of old winding their way over the desert by night, and others who navigated their way by the stars.

Polaris has been known by many names in the past—the Lodestar, the Steering Star, the Ship Star, and *Stella Maris* ("Star of the Sea"). In China it was known as the Emperor of Heaven. It was also known as *Tou Mu*, Chinese goddess of the North Star, so important to those of the Taoist faith. It is believed that *Tou Mu* has the power to prolong life

and that if one prays hard enough to her, the prayers will be answered. Greek navigators of old called Polaris *Kynosoura*, which means the "Dog's Tail." The name came into our English language as *cynosure*, which means "something that strongly attracts attention by its central position."

In Scandinavian mythology the Norse gods made the Universe out of the bits and pieces of the hacked-up bodies of their defeated enemies. To finish the job they hammered an enormous spike, called *Veralder Nagli*, or "World Spike," into the center of the Universe and made the sky revolve about it. The end of the spike had a jeweled nail-head, which remains forever fixed on the great sky dome as Polaris. The Arabs of old regarded Polaris as a hole in the sky in which Earth's axis found its bearing. Like the Norsemen, the Moguls looked on Polaris as holding the Universe together. They called it the Golden Peg. Astronomers of India called Polaris the Pivot of the Planets.

In spite of Polaris's usefulness in navigation, the Arabs looked on the star as an evil star, calling it

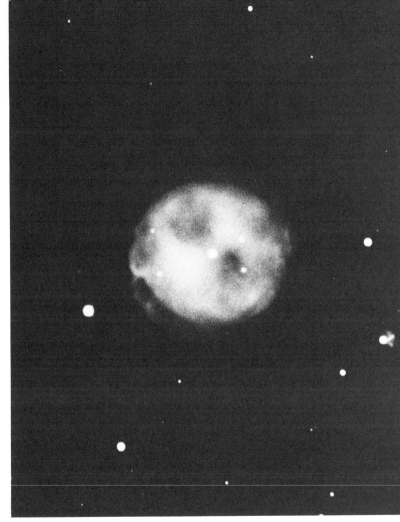

This splendid spiral galaxy (M 81, or NGC 3031), as photographed through the 200-inch telescope, can be seen in Ursa Major. See constellation diagram and star chart for the north polar sky. HALE OBSERVATORIES.

This is the "Owl" Nebula (M 97, or NGC 3587) in Ursa Major, as seen through the 60-inch telescope. See constellation diagram and star chart for the north polar sky for location. HALE OBSERVATORIES.

Al Kiblah, because it was the star "least distant from the pole." It was Polaris, they said, who had slain the great warrior of the sky who forever lies in the huge coffin outlined by the stars marking the Big Dipper. All the other stars mourn for their lost hero and each night march slowly around the sky in a never-ending funeral procession. The villain, Polaris, alone is kept motionless, an outcast forever fixed to the coldest part of the northern sky.

In India there is a myth explaining how the Pole Star came into being as *Dhruva Lok,* or "the Place of Dhruva." Dhruva, the story goes, was a young boy who lived with his mother at the edge of the dark forest. When he was nine years old he asked his mother: "Why does my father not live with us? And why must we live by the edge of this dark forest?"

His mother answered with sadness: "Your father is King of the Land and lives with his new wife in a great palace far away in the city."

"I wish to visit him," said Dhruva. "Tell me how to find him."

She did, and several days later young Dhruva arrived at the great Palace and found his father, the King, who was very happy to see his son.

When Dhruva told his father that he wanted to come and live with him, the King was delighted. But before he could say anything, his jealous second wife stormed into the room and threatened to have Dhruva killed unless the King sent him away immediately. Dhruva left in tears, wondering why his father had not acted strongly. When he told his mother of what had happened, he asked her where he was to find strength since his father was so weak and powerless, although he was King of the Land.

Dhruva's mother said that she knew of only one who could give her son the strength he desired, the Lotus-eyed. But he was a god and she did not know where Dhruva could find him, unless it was in the deepest part of the dark forest where tigers and other fierce beasts dwell. Dhruva set out, determined to find the Lotus-eyed. For three days and three nights he made his way through the thick branches until he felt sure that he must be in the heart of the forest. So he sat down and patiently waited for the Lotus-eyed to appear. Before long he heard a sound and, looking up, saw a figure.

"Are you the Lotus-eyed?" he asked politely, hardly daring to breathe.

"No, I am Narada, Sage of the Forest," the figure replied. "If it is the Lotus-eyed you seek, my son, you must pray to him. You must pray and think of him so hard that nothing else exists for you, neither sky, nor forest, nor the wild beasts inhabiting it." With that, Narada vanished.

Dhruva knew that he had been speaking to one of India's seven wise men who dwell in the seven stars of Ursa Major. Dhruva prayed as hard as he knew how, so hard that nothing else existed for him, not even time itself. After many centuries— exactly how long, no one knows—Dhruva came to realize that he had found the Lotus-eyed. The Lotus-eyed existed in Dhruva's heart. Now Dhruva was contented. He knew that he had the strength he desired. Nevertheless, he forever remained at prayer in deep meditation, for he had discovered

the Lotus-eyed and would never abandon him. A light shone from his heart and so motionless did he remain that all the heavens turned about him. The young Prince, Dhruva, had become *Dhruva Lok*, the Pole Star.

To our eyes, Polaris appears to be motionless at the center of the field of circumpolar stars. All the other stars appear to circle about Polaris. But as early as 320 B.C. the Greeks had realized that Polaris did not mark the pole exactly. Until then many peoples had believed that the heavenly pole was absolutely and eternally fixed. Not so. Polaris has long been moving nearer to the North Celestial Pole, as it is still doing now. It will be closest to that position around A.D. 2100.

Because Earth wobbles on its axis like a slowly spinning top, the Pole Star once was Thuban, the third star from the end of the tail in Draco, the Dragon. And, in a little more than 5,000 years from now, Alderamin, the brightest star in the constellation Cepheus, the King, will be the Pole Star. And then, about 7,000 years from now, Deneb, the brightest star in Cygnus, the Swan, will be the Pole Star for a while. There are long periods when there is no Pole Star at all. But for the time being Polaris occupies the honored place, or very nearly so. It lies some 680 light-years away, one light-year being 10 trillion kilometers (6 trillion miles). At the present time there is no Pole Star in the southern sky. On page 178 we will have more to say about why Earth has changing Pole stars.

> Onward the kindred Bears, with footsteps rude,
> Dance round the Pole, pursuing and pursued.
>
> —ERASMUS DARWIN

URSA MINOR
(the Lesser Bear, or Little Dipper) ☆☆☆☆☆☆☆☆☆☆☆☆☆☆
URSA MAJOR
(the Great Bear, or Big Dipper) ☆☆☆☆☆☆☆☆☆☆☆☆☆☆☆

The Big Dipper is not a constellation by itself. It is part of the constellation of the Great Bear. The seven stars making up the Little Dipper, or Lesser Bear, are much fainter than the seven stars making

The stars of the north circumpolar sky appear to revolve about the North Celestial Pole as shown by this time exposure. LICK OBSERVATORY.

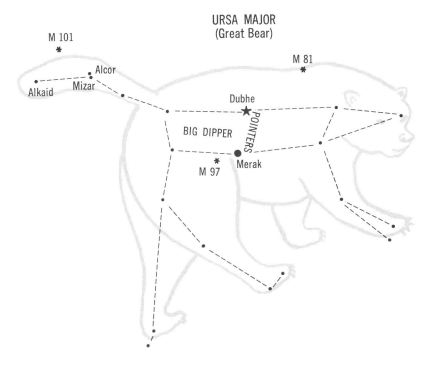

URSA MAJOR
(Great Bear)

up the Big Dipper, which is the most prominent group of stars in the sky.

According to Greek mythology, here is how the Lesser Bear and the Great Bear came to be. Zeus, King of the Gods, fell in love with the beautiful Callisto, a young woman who was a hunter and spent much of her time in the mountains of Arcadia where there was much game. When Hera, Zeus's wife, heard of what was happening she was furious and set out after Callisto. On finding her, Hera said, "Your beauty, of which my husband speaks so tenderly, is no more!" Whereupon Hera changed Callisto into a bear.

To make matters even worse, as Hera was quite capable of doing—as you will find later on, in several other Greek myths involving her—Hera left Callisto with her human feelings rather than those of a bear. So Callisto roamed the forest day and night in constant fear of the hunters *and* in fear of other wild beasts, although she was now one.

One day she found herself face-to-face with a young and handsome hunter and suddenly recog-

nized him as her son, Arcas. She raised up on her hind legs to embrace him. Thinking that the bear was about to attack him, Arcas raised his spear and was about to hurl it and kill his mother. But Zeus happened to be looking down on the scene from his position on Mt. Olympus and instantly turned Arcas into a bear also. Zeus then grasped each bear by its tail and tugged and tugged until he had managed to lift both high into the sky, Callisto as Ursa Major and her son Arcas as Ursa Minor. As the Roman poet Ovid put it, Zeus

> . . . snatched them through the air
> In whirlwinds up to heaven and fix'd them there;
> Where the new constellations nightly rise,
> And add a lustre to the northern skies.

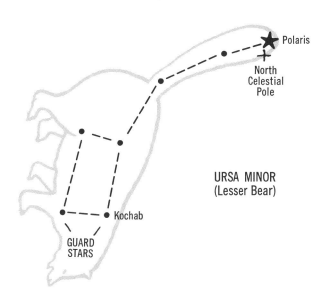

Polaris

North Celestial Pole

URSA MINOR
(Lesser Bear)

Kochab

GUARD STARS

This tugging of tails, by the way, over such a long journey through the sky, stretched both tails and explains why our celestial bears, unlike earthly ones, have long tails. In time, the tail of Arcas became even longer, we are told, since he was continuously swung around the sky by the end-star in his tail, Polaris.

On discovering that her husband had given Callisto and Arcas honored places in heaven, Hera was furious. She went down to Earth to visit her friends the ocean god Oceanus and his wife Tethys. "How dare Zeus give these two an honored place in heaven?" Hera fumed. "They have now displaced me, Queen of Heaven, from my place in the sky. I ask that you forever keep these two in a pen so that they may never wander far."

Oceanus and Tethys were sympathetic and promised they would grant Hera her wish. They would see to it that "the couple never would be permitted to enter our waters in their wandering," in other words, that the bears forever would be forbidden to set below the horizon of the sea as other constellations do. To this day both the Lesser Bear and the Great Bear are held high in the sky near the Pole Star, never permitted to sink beneath the sea horizon.

Another story has it that Ursa Major grew greedy in her old age and wanted to steal the Pole Star for herself since Polaris matches her own stars in brightness. She has never managed to do so, however, because of the "Guard Stars" in Ursa Minor. These two stars form the front edge of the Little Dipper and are located between Polaris and the greedy Great Bear, so protecting Polaris.

The North American Indians also chose bears for these two northern constellations. They called them *Okuri* and *Paukunawa*, both meaning "Bear." And this was before any contact with Europeans. How different cultures at opposite ends of Earth came to associate bears with Ursa Major and Ursa Minor is hard to understand. Possibly the answer lies in some root Asian myth that worked its way both eastward and westward around the globe.

At least some North American Indian groups did not give their celestial bears absurdly long tails. They regarded the tail stars in Ursa Major as three hunters, or as a hunter with two dogs, tracking down the bear. And the star Alcor was the pot in which the bear was to be cooked. The Housatonic Indians further tell us that the hunt is successful each year. They know, because blood spilled by the bear can be plainly seen each fall when the leaves of the forest turn red.

Among the Blackfoot Indians is a myth explaining how the stars of Ursa Major came to be. The elder daughter of a large family fell in love with a grizzly bear and married him while her brothers were away on a hunting trip. Now this was a very special grizzly bear since he had magical powers. Angry beyond words, the girl's father ordered that the tribe's warriors track down and kill the bear, and they did. While the bear was dying, he gave some of his magic powers to his wife. With these powers she turned herself into a grizzly bear and destroyed the entire village in revenge for her husband's death. She also killed her father and mother.

Then she changed back into her human form and began plotting the death of her young brother and sister. Suspicious and frightened, the two children were very pleased when, down by the river, they met their six brothers just returning from the hunt. When the youngsters told the brothers what had happened, the brothers were horrified. Late that night the six brothers and two youngsters tried to sneak out of the village. They knew that if they stayed they would surely be murdered.

Now the elder sister heard them. She immediately changed herself into a bear and ran after them. When they all realized that the bear-woman was slowly catching up with them, they became frightened. But then the younger brother, who also happened to have certain magic powers, shot an arrow in the direction they were running. Instantly all eight of them were at the place where the swift arrow had landed. But still the bear-woman was catching up. Other feats of magic by the young brother were just as useless. Eventually the bear-woman caught up with them and caught five of

them in her claws. But before she could kill them, the young brother shot eight arrows high into the sky. One by one, each of the children disappeared from the bear-woman's strong grip and became a star in the sky.

The six older brothers and the younger one each became one of the seven stars forming the Big Dipper. The young and very frightened sister became the dim star, Alcor, huddling close by one of her brothers, Mizar.

Several of the bear myths associated with Ursa Major involve a chase. So they reflect the fact that the Great Bear endlessly wheels around the northern sky dome as if trying to escape the hunter and dogs pursuing him. Or the bear is in pursuit of the Pole Star, although that star is protected by the Guards of Ursa Minor.

In ancient England, Ursa Major was King Arthur's home and was called Arthur's Chariot. The Irish named Ursa Major after one of their early kings, calling it King David's Chariot. And in France it was the Great Chariot. It has also been called the Wain, the Wagon, and the Plough. Ursa Major, perhaps better than any other group of stars, shows that just about any shape one wants to imagine can be assigned to the constellation—a plough, wagon, coffin, bear, or even a reindeer, as the people of Lapland imagined the constellation.

The brightest star in Ursa Major is the double star Dubhe (magnitude 1.8), from the Arabic *Thahr al Dubb al Akbar*, meaning "the Back of the Great Bear." The second brightest star in the constellation is Merak (mag. 2.4), from *Al Marakk*, meaning the "Loin [of the Bear]."

The brightest-appearing star in Ursa Minor is Polaris (mag. 2), while the second brightest star is the reddish star Kochab (mag. 2.1).

Both Ursa Major and Ursa Minor can be seen throughout the year.

DRACO (the Dragon) ☆☆☆☆☆☆☆☆☆☆☆☆☆☆☆☆☆☆☆☆☆☆☆☆

Draco, the Dragon, is a splendid constellation made up of fifteen or so stars. It is a long figure covering a large part of the northern sky, and in

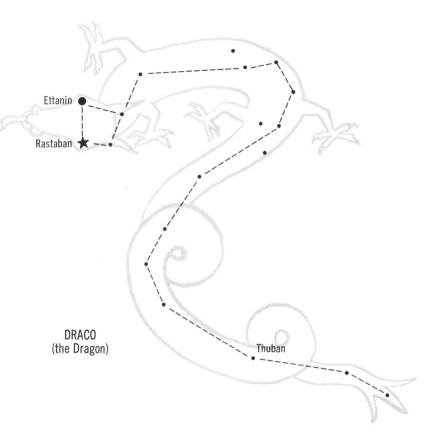

DRACO
(the Dragon)

proper dragon fashion, it twists this way and that. Its head is made up of four stars down near the horizon. Its body then stretches over toward Cepheus, where it twists back in the opposite direction and coils around the Little Dipper, the tip of its tail occupying a position almost in line with the Pointers and Polaris. During August evenings, however, Draco's head is nearly 80° above the horizon.

It's a pity that Draco has so much competition from Ursa Major, Ursa Minor, and Polaris. Although containing mostly faint stars, compared with the brilliance of the Big Dipper, Draco deserves more attention than he usually is given in star identification books. Draco's tail-star, Thuban, was the Pole Star at the time the Egyptian pyramids were being built. You can easily spot Thuban about halfway between Mizar in the handle of the Big Dipper and the Guards forming the front edge of the Little Dipper. The story of Draco's origin is bound to encourage you to look for this fierce monster of the sky.

Dragons abound in myths from many lands. And many of those myths describe how the world was formed, with a dragon playing a star role. Usually, a horrible dragon-monster must be slain by one of the young gods of the new order. The warrior-god, who nearly always is successful in battle, then fashions the Universe out of the hacked-up bits and pieces of the dragon-monster. We cannot be sure which dragon myth is the one associated with the sky dragon, Draco, but one of the earliest such myths handed down to us comes from the ancient Babylonians and the Sumerians before them, some 5,000 years ago. Throughout history, dragons have nearly always been associated with dark, evil deeds. And the Babylonian dragon myth told here is no exception. The myth comes from the *Enuma Elish*, also known as the Babylonian Genesis.

Trouble had erupted among the gods. On the one side were the old gods who had ruled for so long and had become tired and lazy. On the other side was a group of new and younger gods, energetic, wanting to change things, and in search of a new king god. The trouble began when the young gods gathered and danced wildly, whereupon the three old gods in power became angry. One of them, Apsu, says:

Abhorrent have become their ways to me,
I am allowed no rest by day, by night no sleep.

I will abolish, yea, I will destroy their ways,
That peace may reign [again] and we may sleep.

Aware of the plot against them, the young gods formed a Council of Gods which appointed Marduk as the new King God, who was to be armed and sent into battle against Ti'amat, strongest of the old gods. Ti'amat represents the universal and all-powerful sea and can assume whatever form she chooses. The old gods also met in council and drew up their plans to do battle:

Angry, scheming, restless day and night,
They are bent on fighting, rage and prowl like lions.
Gathered in council, they plan the attack,
Mother Hubur—creator of all forms—
Adds irresistible weapons, has borne monster
    serpents,
Sharp toothed, with fang unsparing;
Has filled their bodies with poison for blood.
Fierce dragons she has draped with terror,
Crowned with flame and made like gods,
So that whoever looks upon them shall perish with
    fear.

This woodcut from *Della Tranutatione Metallica*, by Giovanni Battista Nazari, made in 1599, is a reminder of the many dragon-monsters of darkness and evil spawned by the fierce Ti'amat in preparation for her battle with Marduk.

Among the hideous creatures prepared by Mother Hubur were terrifying fish-men, scorpion-men, serpent-men, and goat-men, creatures we will meet many times as we explore the constellations. The most hideous of the monsters by far was the dragon-form which Ti'amat herself had assumed. So terrifying were these transformed gods of chaos that all of the young gods to do battle at Marduk's side fled at the sight of them and hid trembling in the safety of Heaven. Marduk was left alone to meet the enemy.

First he slew the scorpion-monster, then all the remaining ones, leaving the field of battle littered with severed limbs and pools of poison that had dripped out of the bodies of the defeated army of loathsome creatures.

By this time Marduk was exhausted, but he knew he must now do battle with the fierce Ti'amat, who had been all the while looking on and was fresh for battle. Marduk summoned up all the magical powers given him by the other gods and sped to the attack. First he hurled his great net and enclosed

Ti'amat in it. Her great jaws sprung open, tearing the net to shreds. But just as she was about to swallow Marduk, net and all, Marduk commanded the wind to blow with hurricane force and so hold the hideous monster's jaws locked open. Then he fired an arrow through her mouth and into her heart, killing her. Next he mashed her skull, thoroughly bled her, and finally cut her body into two pieces. One half of Ti'amat he raised up toward the heavens and with it formed the sky. With other bits and pieces he set the stage for a calendar by creating the constellations and regulating their periods of apparent rising and setting, as he did for the Sun and Moon.

So that people would never forget the fierce battle waged to create an orderly world out of the forces of chaos, Marduk placed the dragon form of Ti'amat—Draco—in a prominent place in the northern sky. Marduk had well fulfilled his role as the King God and was admired by gods and man alike. Thereafter he was called the Dragon Slayer.

According to a Greek myth accounting for Draco,

once there were several nymphs—lesser goddesses in the form of beautiful maidens. They were daughters of the mighty god Atlas and were known as the Hesperides. They lived in the garden of Hera, Queen of Heaven. It was an unusual garden in that it had a grove of trees that bore golden apples. The nymphs' duty was to guard the golden apples, but so tempted were they by the beautiful fruit that they began to steal some for themselves. When Hera learned of this she sent the ever-watchful dragon, Ladon, a fearsome monster with a hundred heads, to coil around the trees and guard them from the nymphs and others who might be tempted to steal the apples. Meanwhile, Heracles (also known as Hercules) had been given twelve labors to perform so that he might be forgiven for murdering his children in a fit of madness. One of Heracles' tasks was to steal the golden apples of Hera. To do so, he first had to slay Ladon, which he did. Ladon eventually was given immortality in the sky in the form of Draco, the Dragon.

But there is another Greek myth accounting for Draco. As in Babylonian mythology, early Greek myths tell of a great battle between the young gods and the older ones who had ruled for so very long. The new gods included Zeus, together with his brothers Poseidon and Hades. There were also Hera and Demeter along with Athena and others. Athena was the virgin Goddess of Arts, Crafts, and War. Among the older gods associated with evil and darkness was the many-headed monster known as Hydra. There were also other terrifying figures cast up out of the volcanic fires that belched out of the bowels of Earth. These monsters, who represented the universal forces of evil, were known as the Giants, or the Titans.

During the battle, which lasted for ten long years, one of the Giants hurled a fierce dragon at Athena. So great was her strength, however, and so effective her magic shield, that Athena was not frightened. She caught the dragon and, with one mighty heave, swung him high into the heavens. Up he soared, twisting and coiling this way and that until his long body had become tied in knots. He came to rest in the northern sky and became fixed to that region around which the northern stars circle. Today we see him forever asleep as the much-knotted, battered, and twisted Draco.

Draco has also been identified as the Old Serpent, the tempter of Eve in the Garden of Eden. The Persians have regarded Draco as a man-eating serpent called *Azhdeha*, while in early Hindu worship, Draco is given the form of an alligator known as *Shi-shu-mara*.

Before we leave Draco, we should mention this rather interesting fact about its sometime Pole Star, Thuban. The great Egyptian pyramid of Khufu, located at Gizeh, seems to have been planned and built with Thuban as a guide when Thuban was the Pole Star around 3000 B.C. The pyramid was built in such a way that Thuban was visible day and night from the bottom of one of the pyramid's deep shafts. Other pyramids also seem to have been planned and built with the then Pole Star Thuban as a focal point. There must have come a time, however, when the old astronomer-priests of Egypt began to realize that Thuban was not always the Pole Star. As the years passed, and as future generations of astronomer-priests took over, they would have noticed Thuban gradually easing its way out of view up through the telescopelike shaft. And later still, other generations of astronomer-priests would have seen an impudent newcomer slip into view. In this way it could be learned that the Pole Star changes over the centuries. The Egyptians may well have been aware of the changing Pole Star long before the Greeks' mention of it in 320 B.C. But then the Egyptians must have been aware of the fact that their pyramids could be shifted slightly this way and that due to earthquakes, and other forces that reshape Earth's crust.

The brightest star in Draco is the double star Eltanin (magnitude 2.2), located in the monster's head. Thuban (mag. 3.6), in Draco's tail, competes for the number two position in brightness with the head-star Rastaban (mag. 3.0). Draco can best be found in the night sky from late May to early November.

CEPHEUS *(the King)* ☆☆☆☆☆☆☆☆☆☆☆☆☆☆☆☆☆☆☆☆☆☆☆

CASSIOPEIA *(the Queen)* ☆☆☆☆☆☆☆☆☆☆☆☆☆☆☆☆☆☆

It is difficult to tell the story of Cepheus and Cassiopeia without including four other constellation figures intimately involved with them.

The principal characters in this Greek myth include a king (Cepheus), his jealous and boastful wife (Cassiopeia), their very beautiful daughter (Andromeda), a brave young warrior (Perseus), a sea-monster (Cetus), and a winged-horse (Pegasus). Here is how their lives intertwined and how they came to be given honored places among the stars.

Cepheus was an African, the King of Ethiopia, and the beautiful Cassiopeia was his Queen. Soon after their marriage, Cassiopeia bore her husband a daughter, Andromeda. Even when a young girl, Andromeda possessed a beauty as great as that of her mother. Cassiopeia was vain and boastful. So great was her beauty and that of Andromeda, she said, that it surpassed even that of the sea-nymphs.

When the sea-nymphs overheard Cassiopeia they were very jealous. They complained to Poseidon, God of the Sea, and demanded that Cassiopeia be punished. Poseidon agreed and summoned a terrible sea-monster, Cetus. "Go to the coast of Cassiopeia's land," Poseidon directed, "and lay waste to the land, and kill the people, and kill the cattle."

To the horror of Cepheus and Cassiopeia, Cetus, in the form of a monstrous whale, set upon his mission of destruction and began the slaughter, working his way up and down the coast. The frightened people gathered and pleaded to their king to save them. Cepheus consulted an oracle— one with magical powers who could communicate with the gods when men sought their advice. The oracle told Cepheus that there was only one way to stop the slaughter: "You must offer your daughter Andromeda as a sacrifice." She was to be chained to the rocks on the coast and left there for Cetus to devour. Cepheus was torn with grief, for his people and their property, and for his daughter. He made the bitter choice of sacrificing Andromeda, whereupon she was chained to the rocks and abandoned to await Cetus.

When Cetus discovered the prize awaiting him, he left off his wholesale destruction of the land and began swimming toward the ledge where Andromeda was chained. But then a distant figure appeared in the sky. It was Perseus, the brave son of Zeus and Danae, just returning from a journey during which he had succeeded in killing the dreaded Medusa.

The Medusa once had been a beautiful woman with long and flowing hair. So proud was she of her beauty that she dared compare herself with Athena, the virgin Goddess of Arts, Crafts, and War. On hearing of the woman's boastfulness, Athena turned her into a hideous monster. Where her long beautiful hair had once hung were now writhing and hissing serpents. So hideous was the sight of her that any human or animal who chanced to gaze upon her was instantly turned to stone.

On hearing of the loathsome creature, Perseus's mother asked her son to go and slay the dreaded Medusa. Perseus was a favorite of Athena and the wing-footed Hermes. To aid him in battle with the Medusa, Athena lent Perseus her bright shield and Hermes lent him his winged shoes. So equipped, Perseus set out and flew over sea and land to where the Medusa lived.

The Medusa was sleeping when Perseus arrived. Silently he crept toward her, while not looking at her directly. So bright was Athena's shield that he could clearly see the Medusa's reflection in it and so he backed toward her and with a mighty backhanded blow cut off her head. Then with his eyes closed he seized it and stuffed it into the special sack he had brought along.

Triumphant, Perseus again took to the air to present his prize to Athena. On the way some of the blood from the Medusa's severed head dripped out of the sack and fell into the sea. Poseidon felt the drops, recognized them as the Medusa's blood, and was deeply moved. For Poseidon had been in love with the Medusa when she was a beautiful maiden, before she had been bewitched. Remembering how she once had been, he raised her drops of blood from the sea. Then he mixed them with white foam of the dancing waves and with white sand of the beach and out of them he created the Winged Horse, Pegasus.

It was when Perseus was over the coast of Ethiopia that he noticed Andromeda chained to the rocks by the sea, and not far away he could see Cetus rapidly nearing her. Down he swept to the girl's side. "Why are you thus bound?" he asked, overwhelmed by Andromeda's beauty. Andromeda told him the story of her boastful mother and the advice the oracle had given to her father.

As he listened, Perseus could hear distant thrashing in the water. It was Cetus, his head above the waves, parting the waters with his massive scaled body as he approached the shore. Meanwhile, people had gathered along the shore, having heard reports of the approaching sea-monster. They were terrified by his awful appearance as he churned through the waters toward them. Among those present were Cepheus and Cassiopeia, who was now tearfully embracing her daughter.

Perseus quickly turned to Cepheus and said: "I can save your daughter from the sea-monster, but for my reward I demand Andromeda's hand in marriage, and a kingdom." Cepheus promised Perseus that he would have what he asked for, whereupon Perseus unsheathed his sword and leapt into the air to the attack. One thrust of his sword found a soft spot between the armored scales of the monster. Wounded, it twisted over on its side. Perseus then inflicted another deep cut, and another. Blood now colored the water red and soaked Perseus's winged shoes. Fearful of losing his ability to fly, he alighted on a rock near the shore and waited for the sea-monster to attack again. As it did, Perseus's sword plunged deeply into the monster's chest and found its mark directly through Cetus's evil heart. Slowly the monster slipped beneath the waves, leaving only a pool of slime and blood mixed with sea foam from his thrashing.

It is said that to this day the spring by that shore runs red with the blood that Perseus washed from his hands and winged-shoes.

Joyful beyond words, Cepheus and Cassiopeia led Perseus and Andromeda to their house, where a great feast and celebration were prepared. Among those who gathered were many new friends of Perseus's, those who had witnessed his slaying of the sea-monster. Now, unknown to our hero, Andromeda had been promised in marriage by her father to Phineus, her father's brother. But Cepheus had been too fearful to admit this to Perseus. During the height of the celebration, Phineus appeared to claim Andromeda as his own. Accompanying him were many of his followers, all of them armed. Frightened of the outcome, Cepheus cowardly hid himself, trying to explain to the gods that he, Cepheus, was innocent and that the affair was not of his doing.

Meanwhile, Perseus told Phineus that the gods had altered the course of Andromeda's life and that Phineus had no claim on her now. Andromeda did not want to marry her uncle and was now fearful for Perseus in the battle she knew would follow.

Perseus and his comrades were greatly outnumbered by Phineus's small army, but they bravely withstood the onslaught. Perseus realized that it

was only a matter of time before his loyal friends tired and all would be killed. So, shouting in order that all would hear his warning, and reaching into the sack containing the head of the Medusa, Perseus said: "Let all those present who are my friends shield their eyes until I proclaim that it is safe to look upon the world again." As they did, Perseus withdrew the Medusa's head and held it high.

One of Phineus's lieutenants was just about to plunge his javelin through the chest of a victim when out of the corner of his eye he caught sight of the Medusa's head. Instantly, arm raised and poised to strike, he was turned to stone. Within moments the great hall had become adorned with stone statues of warriors in every possible attitude of battle.

Now, on hearing Perseus's warning to his friends, Phineus was wise enough to turn his head away from Perseus. In doing so he quickly saw the great power Perseus held as he watched his men turned to stone. With his head still turned, Phineus made his way toward Perseus and knelt before him. "All I have is yours for the taking," said Phineus. "I ask only that you spare my life."

"Base coward," answered Perseus, "I will grant you but one thing, and that is that no weapon shall touch you. I want you for myself as a memorial to this shameful event you have caused here." Whereupon, Perseus thrust the Medusa's head to one side so that Phineus got a glimpse of it. Instantly he was turned to stone, his head turned away, his hands outstretched, and hunched forward on his knees begging for mercy.

Perseus and Andromeda were married and led a long, happy life together. Their first-born son, Peres, is said to have given rise to those people who became known as the Persians. When Perseus and Andromeda died, they were given honored places among the stars by the goddess Athena. Cetus, the sea-monster, was there waiting for them and forever chases Andromeda around the sky, but Perseus continues to guard her well. Meanwhile Cepheus and Cassiopeia had died and were likewise given honored places among the stars by Poseidon.

Now, when the sea-nymphs heard of Cassiopeia's reward, which they considered unjust, they complained to Poseidon for so honoring her. Poseidon appeased them by placing Cassiopeia in such a position that for half the night she is seen sitting upright on her throne, but for the other half she is seen hanging upside down in an undignified and uncomfortable position. For that reason she is most always shown tied into her chair.

Poseidon saw to it that his beloved Medusa also was given a place among the stars. To this day she can be seen as the star Algol, which is the second brightest star forming Perseus and is located near his waist and beneath his upraised right arm (see *The Autumn Sky*). Algol is a double star, one member of which eclipses the other about once every three days, so it is said to be an eclipsing binary. Algol's name comes from the Arabic *Ra's al Ghul*, meaning "Head of the Demon." Our word *ghoul*, meaning an evil demon who robs graves and regularly feeds on corpses and other such delicacies, comes from that Arabic name for Algol.

Chinese mythology also gives Cepheus an honored place in the sky, where he is known as Tsao Fu, the famous charioteer of around 950 B.C. At that time there was an emperor named Mu Wang who wanted more than anything else in the world to visit that faraway land known as the Western Paradise, by the great mountain K'uen Lun. This was a sacred land of the gods, although once in a while an especially favored mortal might go there.

The rich gardens of this sacred land have flowers unheard of by mortals, flowers whose fruit are jade, pearls, and precious stones of every color. But there is yet another garden, more precious still, a garden owned by Hsi Wang Mu, Queen of the Fairies. In it grows a peach tree that bears fruit only once every three thousand years. Those privileged to eat of this fruit are raised to gods and live for three thousand years.

Now you can understand why Mu Wang was so desirous of visiting the Western Paradise and eating the peaches of Hsi Wang Mu's garden. So he summoned his charioteer, Tsao Fu, and told him to prepare his eight magnificent horses for the long journey ahead of them. They set out, but were never heard of again on Earth. Since there never has been a trace of them, even to this day, it is believed that Tsao Fu was successful in delivering his master to the magic garden of Hsi Wang Mu. It is further believed that Mu Wang was given the magic fruit and even now lives on the slopes of that sacred mountain. For his reward, Tsao Fu was raised into the heavens where to this day we see him as the stars forming Cepheus.

Cassiopeia has also been known as the Celestial "W" and Celestial "M." The Romans called her the Woman of the Chair. In young children's books the constellation is sometimes called Cassiopeia's Chair. To the Arabs, she was the Lady in the Chair. And, instead of seeing Cepheus, the King, Arabian nomads saw a shepherd, his dog, and his sheep. They regarded Cassiopeia as the dog's mate.

Cepheus is among the oldest constellations in the

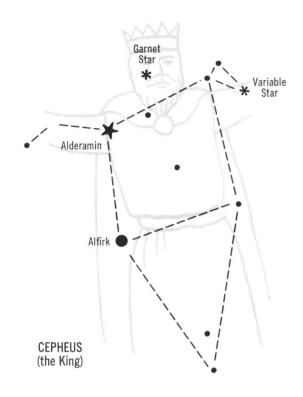

Garnet Star

✳

Variable Star

✳

Alderamin

★

Alfirk

●

CEPHEUS
(the King)

sitting on top. Between the star Alderamin, which marks the King's right shoulder, and the star Al Na'ir, which forms his head, or crown, is a very pretty reddish star called the Garnet Star. It is a variable star that is sometimes a very deep red but which also changes to orange. And as mentioned earlier, the star to the right of Al Na'ir is a prominent variable whose changing brightness you can measure by comparing it with Al Na'ir and the bright star just above, the three forming a triangle.

The brightest star in Cepheus is the white star Alderamin (magnitude 2.4), from the Arabic *Al Deraimin*, meaning "the Right Arm." The second brightest star in this constellation is the double star Alfirk (mag. 3.2).

Cepheus and Cassiopeia both are best observed from August through January.

Queen Cassiopeia occupies a place by her husband's side and is marked by five bright stars shaped as a spread-out "W" or "M." The brightest star in Cassiopeia is Schedar (mag. 2.2 to 2.8), from the Arabic *Al Sadr*, meaning "the Breast." It is a mul-

northern sky and played an important part in Greek mythology. In early Greek times Cepheus was known as the father of the Royal Family. He is not a particularly bright constellation but he is not hard to find, due to his shape—a box with a triangle

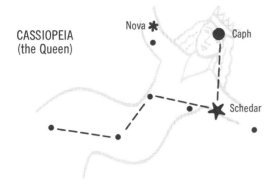

CASSIOPEIA
(the Queen)

Nova

Caph

Schedar

tiple star, slightly variable, and pale rose in color. The second brightest star in this constellation is Caph (mag. 2.3), a white star some forty-five light-years away. In the year 1572 the famous astronomer Tycho Brahe saw a brilliant nova flare up in the position marked on the chart. For nearly two years the nova star remained brighter than Venus and could be seen in the daytime. Then in 1574 it faded from view.

As mentioned earlier, there are a number of interesting sky objects to be seen in and around Cassiopeia (see drawing). The stars of the remaining four constellations making up this larger family will be dealt with in detail on the sky chart of autumn, the season when they are best seen. Except for one

rather dim and uninteresting constellation, called Camelopardalis (the Giraffe), this completes our survey of the north circumpolar sky and the ghosts of the past who live there.

Before leaving this part of the sky, study the diagram on page 47. It will be very useful. It shows how to use the Big Dipper to find a number of individual stars and constellations.

Follow the curve of the handle down and·around to the right and you will find the bright stars Arcturus and Spica. If you follow the two stars forming the inner edge of the Dipper down from the Dipper you will find the bright star Regulus, which forms the chest region of the constellation Leo. Now extend that same line upward above the Dipper and you will find the bright star Vega, one of the three stars forming the famous Summer Triangle (Deneb and Altair being the other two).

Next follow a line from the star forming the top inner edge of the Dipper up through Polaris and it will lead you to the left star in Cassiopeia when she is seen as an "M." Keep going and the line points out the right lower star in the Square of Pegasus, the Winged Horse. Next imagine a line starting from that same star in the Dipper but extending through the lower star forming the outer edge of the Dipper; that line will take you right to Pollux. Pollux is one of the twins in the constellation of Gemini, the Twins.

If you follow the pointer stars right through Polaris and on up, you will find the lower left star in Pegasus. As you can see, not only is the Big Dipper an easy star group to find, but it is a very useful one as well.

> The Big Dipper can be used to help find your way around part of the sky. An imaginary line from Star 1 in the Big Dipper extended through Polaris points to the lower left star in the Square of Pegasus. A line drawn from Star 4 and through Polaris points to the lower right stars in the Square. A line drawn from Star 4 through Star 3 points to Regulus in Leo. A line drawn in the opposite direction through the same two stars points to Vega in the Summer Triangle. A line extended in an arc along the Dipper's handle points first to Arcturus and then to Spica. See how many other ways you can put the Big Dipper to work for you.

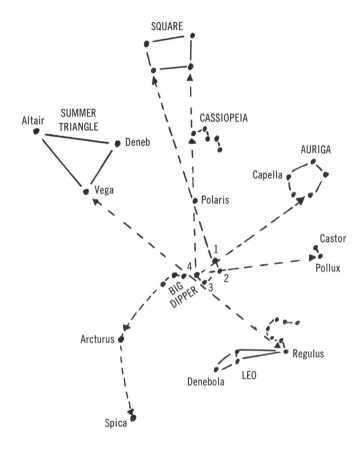

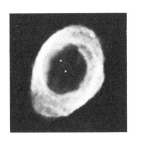

The Summer Sky

The summer sky is especially active, with about a dozen constellations, many particularly bright stars, and several other sky objects that you will be able to see with binoculars or a small telescope.

Among the summer constellations is one that actually looks like the object associated with it—Corona Borealis, or the Northern Crown. And the story about this constellation is an exciting one. Beside the Northern Crown is the huge constellation of Heracles (also Hercules), representing the most famous figure in Greek mythology. Once you have located the well-known trapezoid in Heracles you will be able to locate M 13. Although only a hazy "star" to the eye, actually it is a magnificent globular cluster of stars.

Lyra is another constellation you will want to find because of the very bright and beautiful blue-white star Vega. Lyra also contains the famous Ring Nebula (M 57) and a famous double-double star (Epsilon Lyrae), the one just to the upper left of Vega. But you will need a small telescope to split

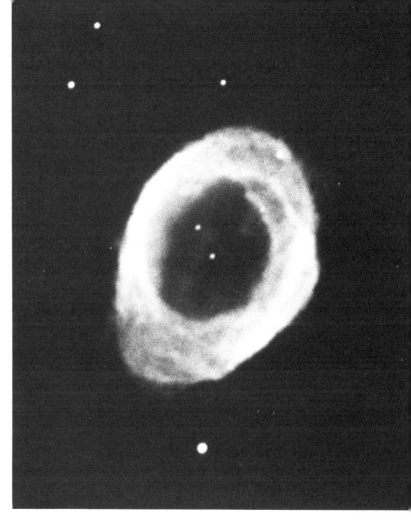

In our galaxy there are about 100 globular clusters like this one (M 13, or NGC 6205) in Hercules, as seen through the 200-inch telescope. Each such cluster contains hundreds of thousands to millions of closely spaced stars. See constellation diagram and the summer star chart (page 50) to locate this cluster. HALE OBSERVATORIES.

This is the famous "Ring" Nebula (M 57, or NGC 6720) in Lyra, as seen through the 200-inch telescope. See constellation diagram and the summer chart (page 50) for location. HALE OBSERVATORIES.

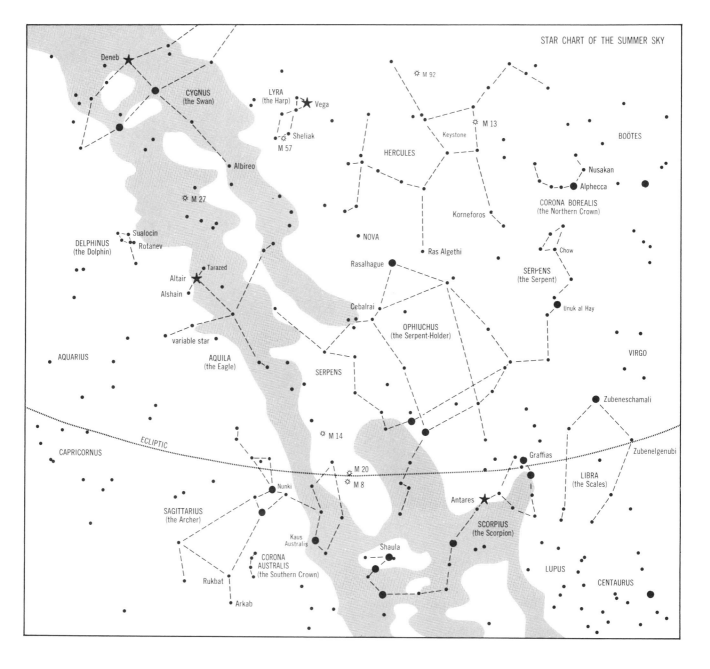

this single-appearing star into its four component stars.

On the opposite side of Lyra from Hercules is Cygnus, the Swan, also known as the Northern Cross. The brilliant white star, Deneb, nearly as bright as Vega, forms the swan's tail. Poised just below Cygnus is Aquila, the Eagle, with its very bright star, Altair, forming the Eagle's head. These three stars—Deneb, Vega, and Altair—form the famed Summer Triangle. Just above and to the left of Aquila is a small constellation, Delphinus, the Dolphin.

Among other notable constellations in the

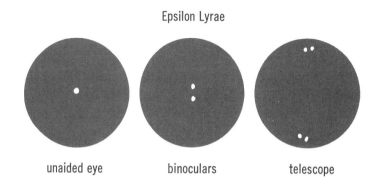

Epsilon Lyrae

unaided eye   binoculars   telescope

This sequence shows what you may expect to see of the famous double-double star Epsilon Lyrae, with the unaided eye, with binoculars, and with a telescope.

The summer star chart shows only those constellation figures mentioned in the text, although numerous additional stars are shown. All star-shaped stars represent stars of magnitude 1.5 and brighter. The large-dot stars represent stars of magnitude 2 to 2.5. The small-dot stars represent stars with magnitudes less than 2.5. Note the long broken line representing the ecliptic. Expect to find planets along and near this ecliptic-line. The light shaded area represents the Milky Way.

summer sky is Ophiuchus, or the Serpent-Holder, which is associated with Serpens, the Serpent. Below Ophiuchus is Scorpius, the Scorpion, which happens to look very much like a Scorpion, complete with a sting-tail star. Scorpius is also a good hunting ground for numerous star clusters and nebulae. To the left of Scorpius is the well-known constellation of Sagittarius, the Archer, another excellent region of the sky to explore for nebulae. Look especially for the Trifid Nebula (M 20), the great Lagoon Nebula (M 8), visible to the naked eye, and the Horseshoe Nebula (M 17). Binoculars will reveal numerous star clusters in this area of the sky.

CYGNUS (the Swan) ☆☆☆☆☆☆☆☆☆☆☆☆☆☆☆☆☆☆☆☆☆☆☆☆

Phaethon was the son of Clymene, whose husband was the Egyptian king Merops. One day Phaethon's mother told him that Merops was not his father, that his real father was the Sun-god Apollo. When Phaethon boasted to his friends that his real father was a powerful god, his friends teased him and said that he was not telling the truth. Hurt, Phaethon questioned his mother, who told him: "Go to the Sun-god and ask him yourself if you doubt my word."

Clymene told Phaethon that he would have to travel far, through Ethiopia and India, in order to find his father's shining palace of gold in the East, at the place where the Sun rises each day. Phaethon set out and many months later reached Apollo's palace. The Sun-god was delighted to see his son and promised Phaethon anything he requested in the way of proving to his friends that Apollo, indeed, was his father.

Phaethon thought for a while and finally said that he wanted permission to drive the Sun-chariot across the sky for one day. Apollo was shocked and tried to convince his son that it was a very dangerous thing to do, in hopes that the boy would reconsider his request. Phaethon refused to change his mind, so there was nothing for Apollo to do but keep his word.

The next day the four fiery horses were harnessed and Phaethon rashly set out. If only he had known of the dangers that lay ahead, dangers that struck fear into the heart of even Apollo himself!

"Make sure to steer a middle course, keeping half-way between Heaven and Earth," Apollo shouted to his excited son. But the boy was too nervous to hear. A flick of the reins sent the horses leaping forward into the sky. Phaethon was inexperienced in driving a chariot and it did not take

The "Trifid" Nebula (M 20, or NGC 6514) in Sagittarius, as photographed through the 200-inch telescope. See constellation diagram and summer star chart for location. HALE OBSERVATORIES.

The "Lagoon" Nebula (M 8, or NGC 6523) in Sagittarius, as photographed through the 200-inch telescope. See constellation diagram and summer star chart for location. HALE OBSERVATORIES.

the horses long to realize that an unsure hand was on the reins. They began galloping wildly, with Phaethon unable to control them. First they bolted high up in the sky, far higher than they usually did, in their eagerness to rise above the eastern horizon and reach the top of the great sky dome. It was here that they scorched a great streak across the sky, a streak that became the Milky Way. Meanwhile Earth's surface became cold because the Sun-chariot was so high in the sky. Next the horses plunged too close to Earth. As they crossed Africa they scorched the ground, creating a great desert and drying up rivers, lakes, and watering holes. It became so hot that all the people in that land were scorched black.

Horrified, Phaethon saw ahead of him a great Scorpion in the sky (see page 82). Its mighty tail flashed and stung the lead horse. Up went the chariot again, even more wildly than before. Poor Phaethon now realized his foolishness, that he should have listened to his father's warning. But now he was lost and he wept, for he could think of nothing else to do.

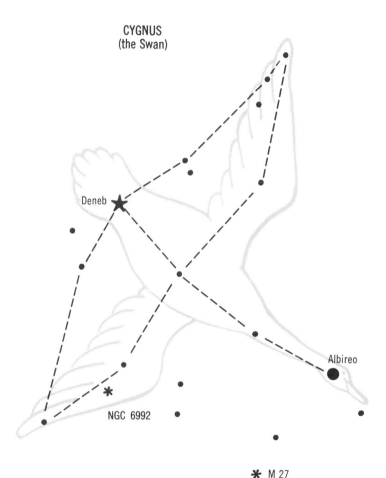

CYGNUS
(the Swan)

Deneb

Albireo

NGC 6992

✳ M 27

Zeus, King of the Gods, had been looking on all the while and decided that it was time to stop this rash youth from causing more destruction. He hurled a thunderbolt at Phaethon, killing the boy instantly and sending his smoldering body tumbling down to Earth. The horses returned to their stable and Phaethon's body eventually fell into the Eridanus River and sank to the bottom. Phaethon's sisters were heartbroken at the loss of their brother and sat by the river crying. They were turned into poplar trees. Even so they continued to drop tears, which now changed into amber and mixed with the sands. And this accounts for the amber so long found mixed with the sands of the beaches along the Eridanus.

Phaethon had a very devoted friend, Cycnus, the Musician-king of the Ligurians. His people lived on the coastal area of northwestern Italy and southern France. On hearing of Phaethon's fate, Cycnus plunged into the Eridanus and swam back and forth, diving repeatedly to try to find the body of his friend. His motions through the water made him look like a swan searching for food. Apollo took pity on Cycnus, who died of grief, and raised him to stardom, where he became the constellation Cygnus, the Swan.

Another version of the myth has Cycnus wandering through the poplar grove grieving and mourning the death of Phaethon until, by the will of Apollo, Cycnus is spared further grief and is raised among the stars. Ever since then swans are said to sing sad songs when they are about to die, hence our expression "swan song." The river Eridanus was also given an honored place in the sky, between Draco and Pegasus, but this constellation does not appear in its full glory until the winter months (see The Winter Sky).

People of several cultures have seen a bird of one kind or another in Cygnus, including a horned owl

The "Veil" Nebula (NGC 6992) in Cygnus, as photographed through the 100-inch telescope. See constellation diagram and summer star chart for location. HALE OBSERVATORIES.

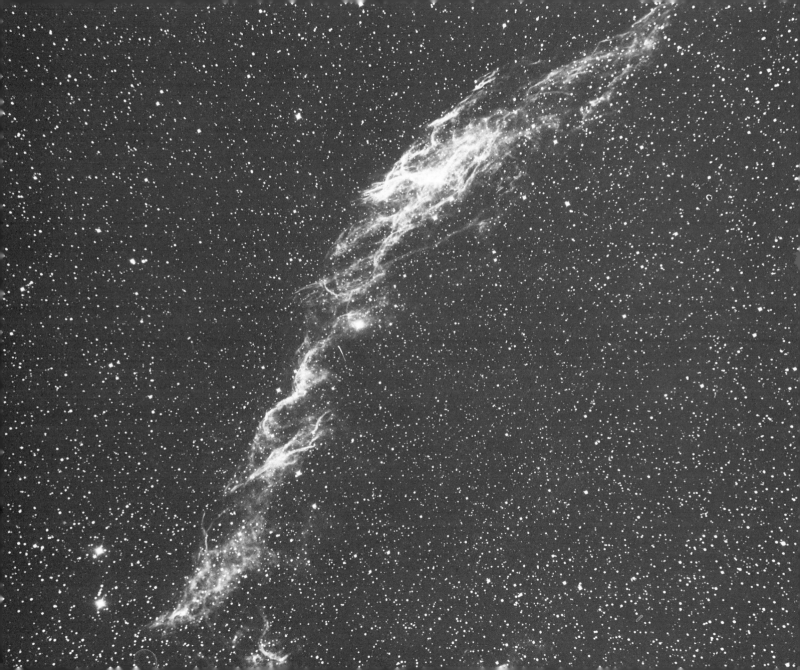

and an ibis. The Arabs have called the constellation *Al Tair al Arduf,* meaning the "Flying Eagle," and *Al Dajajah,* "the Hen." The Egyptians of 300 B.C. also saw a hen in the constellation. On many star charts, Cygnus is shown in full flight down along the Milky Way, that section of sky "scorched" by Phaethon.

Christians during the early Christian era saw a cross rather than a swan, hence the alternate name, Northern Cross:

> Yonder goes Cygnus, the Swan, flying southward,
> Sign of the Cross and of Christ unto me.

The brightest star in Cygnus is Deneb (magnitude 1.3), a white star forming the Swan's tail. The name is from the Arabic *Al Dhanab,* meaning "the Hen's Tail." The second brightest star in this constellation is the beautiful star Albireo (mag. 3.1). See if you can split this double star, one component of which is gold and the other sapphire-blue. The Arabs called the star *Al Minhar al Dajajah,* meaning "the Hen's Back."

Cygnus is best seen from June through November.

LYRA *(the Lyre)* ☆☆☆☆☆☆☆☆☆☆☆☆☆☆☆☆☆☆☆☆☆☆☆☆☆☆

Hermes, Messenger of the Gods, one day came upon an empty tortoise shell on the beach and out of it fashioned a small harplike instrument, the lyre. When in the right hands the instrument produced the most beautiful music ever heard by either gods or mortals. Now Hermes traded his invention with the Sun-god Apollo. Later, Apollo presented the lyre to his son, Orpheus. So gifted was Orpheus at playing the lyre that neither mortals, beasts, nor the gods themselves could turn away when he played. It is said that on hearing Orpheus play, the dark god Pluto, Lord of the Underworld, wept tears of iron, so sweet was the music.

In time Orpheus took a wife, the young and beautiful Eurydice. But soon after their marriage she was bitten by a serpent and died, whereupon she was transported to the Underworld, where all mortal souls went. Now Orpheus himself entered

Hades, playing the lyre as he went. Pluto and all the other ruling spirits were so enchanted by Orpheus's music that they agreed to restore life to Eurydice—but only on one condition—that as Orpheus left Hades he would not look back to see if his wife were following him. Although he agreed, when he was nearly back at Earth's surface he could not understand why he had not heard footsteps behind him if his wife really were there. So, breaking his vow, he looked back. He saw Eurydice, but she rapidly faded away into the mists of Hades. Now she was lost to him forever, for once reborn, a departed soul cannot be reborn a second time.

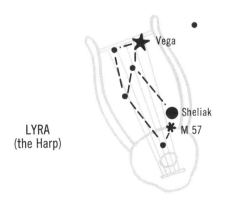

LYRA
(the Harp)

Utterly sad and lonely, Orpheus spent the rest of his days roaming over the land playing sweet but sad music to himself in memory of his dear wife. So sweet was the music that maidens from far and wide came to him and followed him and pleaded that he forget his sorrows and marry one of them. But he would not.

Their pride crushed, the young maidens vowed to kill Orpheus since they could not have him for their own. They tore him apart limb by limb and threw his remains and lyre into the river. Zeus knew of these events. Also enchanted by the sweet music of Orpheus, Zeus rewarded the young man by making his music immortal. He raised the lyre into the skies and placed it beside the graceful swan, Cygnus. A small but brilliant constellation, Lyra is crowned with the bright star Vega, also known as the Harp Star.

The Chinese also have a myth for Lyra. It describes a youth raised by his father, who died as the boy entered manhood. The young man, Tung Yung, loved his father very much, and, as is proper among the Chinese, knew he must give his father a grand funeral and comfortable burial site. For it is Chinese custom that one's attention to the needs of a departed loved one is more important than one's attention when the person is alive. This is to assure that the departed soul is comfortable in his afterlife.

As badly as Tung Yung wanted to give his father a splendid funeral, he could not, for he was very poor. He lived in a small shack and had only wooden planks for a bed. The only way he could honor his father was to sell himself as a slave, which he did. With the money, he provided a splendid funeral and burial, with mourners all dressed in white, a magnificent coffin, gold and silver paper money, and many other things his father would need in his afterlife.

It was now time for the young man to pay off his debt to the wealthy estate owner who had bought him as a slave. After several weeks of hard work from sunrise to sunset each day, Tung Yung soon became ill and his friends feared for his life. The great Lord of Heaven, who had been aware of Tung Yung's devotion to his father, and the resulting hardships he was now suffering, took pity on the young man. He sent his beautiful daughter, Chih Nu, and told her to go down to Earth and look after Tung Yung.

Too ill even to crawl off his wooden bed to feed himself, Tung Yung was startled to open his eyes and see a beautiful maiden smiling down on him. Instantly he recovered. He was a little frightened, for he saw in her manner something that was not earthly. "Who are you?" he asked timidly.

"It is not important," she answered. "I have come from very far away and am now your wife. I will look after you and give you happiness."

Tung Yung was overwhelmed and could not understand why such good fortune had shone upon him. At the end of each day when he returned from the rice fields, he found their hut warm and shining clean and Chih Nu was busy weaving at her loom. Tung Yung had never seen such beautiful silk weaving in his life. Before long, rich people from far and wide came to Tung Yung's hut to bid for the beautiful tapestries woven by his wife. And before long they had enough money to buy Tung Yung his freedom and a large farm with many servants of his own. By this time Chih Nu had borne her husband a son. But before the child was barely a year old, Chih Nu realized that her work was finished and that she must return home and once again take up her duties to her father. Although the gods are permitted to visit Earth and live there for a while as mortals, they must not overstay their visit or they will lose their position as a god.

So it was with great grief and weeping that one night just after her beloved husband and child had gone to sleep Chih Nu left as quickly and mysteriously as she had come. According to the Chinese, to this day she can be seen as the brilliant star Vega, seated at her loom weaving tapestries of such beauty that they are fit only for the gods. The Chinese know her as the Spinning Damsel, or the Weaving Sister.

Once you have found Vega, you will return to the star again and again for another look. At latitudes greater than 52° N it is visible every night of the year. It is a relatively nearby star, only 26.5 light-years distant from us. In about 12,000 years from now Vega will be the Pole Star, and what a brilliant Pole Star it will be, some six times brighter than Polaris.

It seems that the Sumerians and Babylonians saw in Lyra not a harp but a vulture. This is suggested by early Greek records of the constellation as a harp being carried by a vulture. So instead of being the Harp Star it may once have been the Vulture Star. The ancient peoples of Britain called Lyra "the Harp of King Arthur."

Many times throughout this book you will find examples of one group of people borrowing this or that myth from an earlier group and then casting their own heroes in the lead roles. When the Babylonians conquered the Sumerians, they took the old Sumerian myths and provided them with new (Babylonian) heroes. When the Romans conquered Greece, they took over the old Greek myths and provided them with new (Roman) heroes. For this reason, there must always be a grand battle of the gods when one culture conquers and takes over the legends and myths of an older culture. Remember that the new upstart gods of the Babylonians, led by Marduk, had to overthrow the old order of gods represented by Ti'amat. Likewise, Zeus and his followers, a new order of gods, had to overthrow the Giants in a battle that took ten long years. And then still later the Romans demoted Zeus and replaced him with their own King-god Jupiter. They also replaced Hera with Juno, Helios with Apollo, Hermes with Mercury, Athena with Minerva, and so on down the line. Part of the fun in reading the old myths is to see how far back we can trace them, in what significant ways they became changed along the way, and how many different cultures far removed from each other adopted one or more of the myths after tailoring them to their own hero figures and demons.

The brightest star in Lyra is the brilliant blue-white star Vega (magnitude 0.04), whose name comes from the Arabic *Waghi*. It is the brightest star in the summer sky. The second brightest star in this constellation is the intensely white star Sheliak (mag. 3.4), from the Arabic *Al Shilyak*. This is an easily observed variable star with a period of about thirteen days. As mentioned earlier, you will also want to try to split the famous double-double star, Epsilon Lyrae (mags. 4.4 and 5.1), beside Vega, and find the famous Ring Nebula beneath Sheliak.

Lyra is best seen from May through November.

HERACLES (also Hercules) ☆☆☆☆☆☆☆☆☆☆☆☆☆☆☆☆☆☆

Lying to the right of tiny Lyra is the giant but faint constellation Heracles better known as Hercules, about whom an entire book could be written since he is perhaps the most famous figure in Greek mythology, even if he is not the most famous figure in the night sky. Finding Draco will help you find Hercules since one foot is resting on Draco's head. And that alone should tell you something of the might of this sky warrior. Hercules is made up of twenty or more stars and has a history going back thousands of years, a history very little changed through time and having its roots in Sumerian mythology.

Hercules was the son of Zeus, King of the Gods, and the mortal woman, Alcmene. Zeus was famous for going around the countryside disguising himself this way and that and having children by earthly women. Hercules was one such of his many children. When Hercules was only eight months old, Alcmene's real husband, jealous because Hercules was not his own child, placed two serpents in Hercules' crib. The serpents stung Hercules' brother to death, but the infant Hercules grabbed both serpents and strangled them. Such was his strength when only an infant.

When still a boy, Hercules reached a height of more than six feet and had become expert in many manners of combat—wrestling, shooting with bow and arrow, and spear-throwing, to mention but a few. And his great strength already was discussed

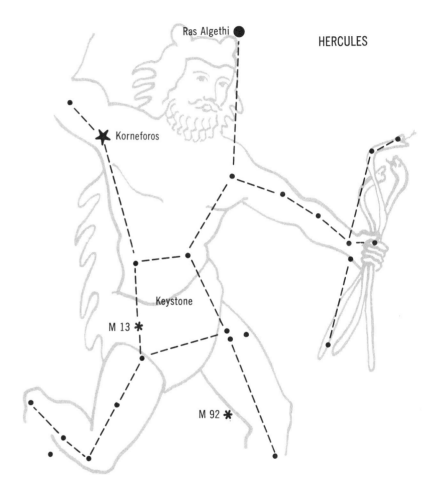

far and wide. Hercules married, had children, engaged in many hair-raising adventures, and fought courageously in war. Hera, Zeus's wife, was still outraged and jealous over Hercules and would not rest until he was dead. It seems that Hera's will to defeat him was so great that she cast a spell of madness over Hercules and caused him to kill his own children, and two children of his nephew, Iolaus.

When Hercules came to his senses and realized the awful thing he had done, he left his homeland in deep sorrow, telling himself he was not fit to live among his people anymore. He asked the advice of an oracle and the reply was, "To be forgiven your crime you must journey to Tiryns and perform whatever twelve labors King Eurystheus demands of you. If you succeed in these labors, whatever they are, you will be raised to the rank of a god." Hercules said that he would do as he was bid.

LABOR 1: Hercules' first labor was to kill the Nemean lion, a fierce beast with hide so tough that neither spear nor arrow nor any weapon could pierce it. So well known was the beast that Hercules had no trouble finding its lair, a cave with two entrances. As Hercules approached, the lion showed itself and Hercules sped an arrow toward its heart. But the arrow merely bounced off and fell to the ground. Hercules now knew that arrows or spears were useless against the beast. He then sealed off one of the entrances to the cave and pursued the lion inside through the other entrance. So great was his strength that Hercules seized the lion and strangled it to death. He then flung it over his shoulder and returned to show King Eurystheus that he had fulfilled his first labor. The cowardly king was terrified at the sight of the beast and fled. Hercules then skinned the lion and used its tough hide as a protective shield.

So angry was Hera at Hercules' success that she raised the soul of the lion high into the sky, where today he can be seen as the constellation Leo, the Lion (see The Spring Sky).

LABOR 2: Hercules next was told that he must kill the dreaded Hydra, an enormous and hideous water serpent with nine heads. One of the heads was immortal and could not be killed. It is said that Hera had nourished the Hydra out of hatred for Hercules, knowing that one day Hercules would engage the monster in deadly combat. Hercules had no trouble finding the Hydra and coaxing it out of its den. The Hydra sprang to the attack and wrapped itself around Hercules' arms, legs, and body. Hercules hacked this way and that and thrust his sword into any part of the Hydra he managed to strike. He became troubled on finding that one of the monster's heads simply bounced away from his sharp sword, and that each time he hacked off one of its heads two more grew in its place.

Hercules realized that he must use some new form of attack. For not only did he have to battle the Hydra, but Hera had sent to the Hydra's defense an enormous crab to bite Hercules about the feet and arms. Hercules' mighty sword quickly hacked the crab to pieces, but the Hydra simply became more ferocious and deadly with each wound Hercules was able to inflict. Then Hercules had an idea. With all his might he called to one of his friends and told him to bring torches blazing with the fiercest flames. When the torches arrived, Hercules seized one and on cutting off a head of the Hydra immediately burned the stump of the neck. This prevented two new heads from growing where there had been one. Head after head was hacked off and each neck-stump burned until only the immortal head was left. This one Hercules hacked off far down on the neck and buried it beneath a huge rock where it could do no harm even though it was immortal. Before leaving the Hydra, Hercules dipped the tips of many of his arrows into the monster's poisonous blood. These arrows were to become very useful later, and one of them was to play a part in his own death.

Once again Hera was furious because she had not been able to kill Hercules with the dreaded Hydra or the ferocious Crab. So, as she had done with the lion, she elevated these two creatures into the sky where to this day we can see them as Cancer, the Crab, and as Hydra, the Many-headed Monster.

Triumphant, Hercules returned to King Eurystheus. But the King refused to let Hercules claim this victory as one of his labors because he had summoned help and had not performed the labor alone.

LABOR 3: Eurystheus next commanded Hercules to capture and deliver to him alive the fabled Cerynitian hind, a deer with antlers of solid gold—a sacred pet of Artemis, Goddess of Wild Animals. It is said that Hercules pursued the elusive and swift animal for a year before he managed to run it down and capture it unharmed and carry it on his shoulders to the King.

LABOR 4: Hercules was next told to return to the land of Arcadia, from which he had just come, and to capture alive the Erymanthian boar. The boar was a huge beast that roamed and ravaged the countryside. Its hide was too thick to pierce with a spear or arrow and its vicious snout was like a thousand spears and knives whirling as a hurricane. Hercules pursued the beast, craftily forcing it ever higher up the slope of a mountain. Eventually they came to snow and still higher he forced the beast. Finally it became bogged down in the deep snow and was helpless to defend itself. Hercules then bound its head to its chest and carried it alive back to the King.

LABOR 5: So great were King Eurystheus's fears of the prizes brought back by Hercules that the King each time hid himself in a great jar buried in the ground. As Hercules succeeded in each task, the King became angrier and angrier and tried to think up a labor that Hercules could not possibly fulfill. To give himself time to ponder the problem, Eurystheus gave Hercules a "fill-in" task, one he hoped would so shame Hercules that he would give up his quest for immortality. Hercules' fifth labor was to clean out the stables of King Augeas, of Elis, which held 3,000 oxen. The stables had not been cleaned for thirty years, and Hercules was given but one day to perform the labor. He said that he would do it if the King would pay him one-tenth of the cattle in return.

An agreement was made, whereupon Hercules

dug great ditches in the land and changed the courses of two rivers in such a way that they flowed right through the stables, scouring them clean in one day. Again Hercules returned to his king, successful in his labor. The King scoffed and said that this labor could not possibly count because Hercules had entered into a financial deal as payment for his task.

LABOR 6: This time Hercules was told to go to Arcadia and chase away the Stymphalian birds, loathsome creatures that ate men and shot their feathers like darts into mortals, killing them. The land was overridden with the birds, Hercules was told. So he went to Arcadia, armed with a magic rattle given to him by Athena. From atop a mountain near a lake where the greatest number of the birds lived, he sounded the rattle and the birds took flight. Hercules then shot a great number of the remaining birds and all the rest flew away.

LABOR 7: Eurystheus next said that Hercules must capture alive and deliver to him the fearsome Cretan bull. Now this beast lived far away in a foreign land, and it is said that Eurystheus was becoming nervous with the triumphs of Hercules. So nervous was the King that he now began to send Hercules to far ends of Earth to accomplish his tasks, in hopes that he would never return.

Hercules set off on his new venture with more determination than ever of returning with his prize, and he did.

LABOR 8: Hercules next had to travel far and capture the four mares of Diomedes. Diomedes was a savage king whose mares fed only on human flesh. On arriving in the king's distant land Hercules overpowered the grooms guarding the mares and drove the animals down to the sea. At the shore the mares became restless because they had not been fed for two days. At the moment Hercules was trying to control them, Diomedes himself appeared and attacked Hercules. Holding the four leaping and snorting mares by their bridles in one hand, Hercules swiftly hacked Diomedes in two with his sword. He then hacked up the body and fed it to the mares, who then calmed down and let Hercules lead them to King Eurystheus.

LABOR 9: Annoyed at one success after another, Eurystheus set for Hercules a labor that surely would be impossible to accomplish: to journey to the faraway land of the Amazons. The Amazons were a fierce, warlike tribe of huge women who lived by the southern shore of the Black Sea. Hercules' task was to visit these women and return with the belt of their queen, Hippolyte. Hercules arrived in their land by boat and asked to speak to Hippolyte, and his wish was granted. She came aboard his ship and so taken with him was she that she agreed to let him have her belt.

Now Hera was looking down on the scene, as always, and was furious to see that Hercules was getting his own way with no resistance from Hippolyte. So she disguised herself as an Amazon and swooped down into the midst of them. She then quickly convinced them that Hercules was in the process of kidnapping their queen. Instantly the women armed themselves and attacked the ship. Now Hercules thought that Hippolyte had tricked

him and instantly killed her and snatched her belt, which he delivered to King Eurystheus.

LABOR 10: Hercules next was told that he must travel to the distant land of Erytheria and bring back the cattle of Geryon. Now Geryon was the king of Erytheria and was said to have three heads. His cattle were watched over by one Eurytion who had a two-headed watchdog named Orthus.

After his long journey overland and voyage by sea, Hercules reached the land of Erytheria where he was met by Eurytion and Orthus. They were no match for Hercules who easily did them in with his club. Hercules rounded up the king's cattle and was about to leave with them when the king himself came rushing out toward Hercules. One arrow hit its mark and Geryon was no more. Hercules had many hair-raising adventures on his way home before successfully delivering the cattle of Geryon to King Eurystheus.

LABOR 11: The golden apples of the Hesperides were guarded by a fierce dragon, Ladon. And the apples belonged to none other than Hera, Hercules' bitterest foe. What more fitting task, thought Eurystheus, than to send Hercules into the arms of Hera. You can find out how Hercules carried out this labor by reading the story of Draco, the Dragon, back on page 36. But we must tell of two of the several adventures that Hercules had in the course of fulfilling his mission.

At one stage when he was traveling westward through Libya, Hercules visited King Antaeus, a son of Gaea (Earth). Now, Antaeus amused himself by challenging strangers to a wrestling match. And his reputation far and wide was that he had killed every one of his opponents. The match began and Hercules had no trouble throwing Antaeus down the first time, the second time, and the third time. But he became puzzled as he noticed that each time he threw Antaeus to the ground, the king seemed refreshed and became stronger. After several more falls and the gaining of renewed strength, Hercules realized that Antaeus's mother, Earth, was responsible and gave her son new strength each time Antaeus touched the ground. Whereupon

Hercules snatched Antaeus off the ground, held him in the air, and crushed him in his arms in a great bear hug. Hercules was to turn to his wits still another time before he completed his mission.

Eventually Hercules came to the very spot where the great Atlas stood, balancing the sky on his massive shoulders. Ah-ha, thought Hercules. Why not persuade Atlas to steal the golden apples while I temporarily relieve him of his great burden? Atlas was only too happy to be relieved of the heavy sky and agreed to slay the dragon who guarded the Hesperides who guarded the golden apples of Hera. Even for the mighty Hercules the task of supporting the sky was very difficult and he was delighted when Atlas returned with the apples and placed them on the ground near Hercules.

But Atlas had no intention of putting the sky back on his shoulders for eternity now that he was rid of it. So he offered to take the golden apples to King Eurystheus.

Hercules knew that he had been tricked and realized that he must think fast to get out of this one. "This is a splendid idea," he said to Atlas, pretending to agree. "You deserve a rest from this task of tasks. Yes, you deliver the golden apples to Eurystheus and then return. But before you go," Hercules continued, hoping that his trick would work, "will you please hold the sky for a moment so that I can put a soft pad on my head?"

The dim-witted giant agreed, and as soon as Hercules was free of the burden he scooped up the golden apples and was on his way. (This version of the myth differs from the version told in the section about Draco, where it is Hercules himself who kills Ladon and takes the apples.)

When he returned home and presented the golden apples to Eurystheus, the King was terrified because now he was the owner of property stolen from the powerful goddess Hera. So Eurystheus instantly gave the golden apples to Hercules. Hercules didn't want the stolen property either, so he took the apples directly to the goddess Athena. Athena promptly returned them to the garden of Hera to be watched over by the Hesperides.

LABOR 12: Eurystheus realized that this was his last chance to defeat Hercules, so he chose the most difficult task left to his imagination. "Bring me the Cerberus from Hades as your final labor," he told Hercules. Now the Cerberus was a dreaded hound with three (some say fifty) heads and a serpent's tail, and it guarded the gates to Hades. The Cerberus was brother to the many-headed Hydra, to the hound Orthus, and to the Nemean lion, all of which Hercules had slain.

With the god Hermes as his guide, Hercules descended to the Underworld and entered Hades. Phantom spirits slipped past him this way and that through the gray, cold mists that swirled about him in the dim light. Suddenly he saw the Medusa come toward him through the fog and quickly drew his sword. "It is only a phantom," Hermes said, "you need not worry. There are only phantoms here."

Soon he met Hades, God of the Underworld, and Hercules said that he was going to carry off Cerberus. One version of the myth says that Hades agreed, if Hercules could overcome the beast without the use of weapons. Hercules agreed, and after a fearsome wrestling match that struck terror even into the souls of the dead who witnessed the match, Hercules dragged the submissive beast out of Hades and into the light above. When he dropped the quivering Cerberus at the feet of King Eurystheus, the King shrieked, "Take it back! Take it back!" Hercules obeyed.

This completed the twelve labors of Hercules. Now the oracle had said that if Hercules succeeded in his labors he would be raised to the rank of a god, but it had not said when. As it came to pass, Hercules had many more years to live on Earth as a mortal before gaining immortality, and his adventures over those years were every bit as violent as any he had experienced during his twelve labors. Further, Hera, still his bitter enemy, vowed to cast spells of madness over him whenever she could and cause him to do more evil deeds for which he would have to perform still more labors in order to be forgiven.

During one of his adventures, Hercules commanded a fleet of Greek ships and had just defeated the Trojans under Laomedon. His success so infuriated Hera that she caused violent winds to blow the Greek vessels many miles off their course. Now Zeus was aware of Hera's many deeds against his son Hercules. And this last act of hers made him so angry that he hung her by her wrists and attached heavy weights to her feet. And there he let her swing until it suited him to untie her.

The other gods, too, looked kindly on Hercules. One reason was that at this time they were waging battle against the Giants, and it was written that the gods could not put down the enemy without the help of one mortal. Clearly, Hercules was that mortal. When asked to help them in battle, Hercules willingly did and bravely fought side by side with Apollo and many of the other gods, in the process slaying several of the Giants. His task completed, Hercules returned to his own earthbound life.

Eventually he abandoned his first wife, saying that the gods must have wished him to since they had made him kill his own children. Therefore, the marriage must be an unlucky one. So he took a new wife, Deianeira, daughter of King Oeneus of Calydon. On one of their journeys together, they came to a broad river which they had to cross. A centaur named Nessus had become rich by ferrying travelers across the river. Now Nessus hated Hercules because the centaur, along with his friends, had many years earlier been driven from Arcadia by Hercules (see page 88). Hercules did not recognize Nessus and said that only his wife, Deianeira, would need help crossing the river.

When halfway across, Hercules, swimming by himself, looked back to find that Nessus was rapidly swimming downstream away from Hercules. When the centaur reached the shore he began to attack Deianeira, who was screaming for Hercules' help. As soon as his feet touched bottom, Hercules drew his bow and killed the centaur with one of his poisoned arrows. The arrow tip long ago had been dipped into the poisonous blood of the Hydra slain by Hercules. Before Hercules arrived on the scene,

the dying Nessus, still plotting against Hercules, told Deianeira to soak up some of his spilled blood and save it, for it would act as a love charm if Hercules should ever begin to stray from her. All she would have to do was rub some of the blood on a garment of Hercules and he would love only her. Now Deianeira foolishly believed the dying centaur and did as she was instructed before Hercules could see what was happening.

Years later, indeed, Deianeira did become jealous of her husband, although she had no need to. When Hercules was away on an expedition and sent to her for fresh garments to wear, she smeared one of the garments with the poisoned blood of the centaur. As soon as Hercules put it on the poison burned into his flesh with terrible pain. When Hercules tore the garment from his body his flesh came away with it. By now the poison had soaked well into his body and he was beyond help.

In great pain, Hercules made his way home. When Deianeira discovered what she had done, she was so horror-stricken that she killed herself.

A cluster of galaxies in Hercules, as seen through the 200-inch telescope. HALE OBSERVATORIES.

Hercules, accompanied by friends, made his way to the top of Mount Oeta. There they built a small platform of wood and beneath it placed heaps of branches and logs. Hercules climbed onto the platform and fire was set to the wood. Soon flames and smoke engulfed the dying Hercules, and then suddenly a lightning bolt struck into the heart of the cloud enclosing him. When the smoke cleared there were no remains of their hero, not even an ash.

Hercules had at last, after much suffering, attained the rank of a god. His twelve labors complete, he could at last rest in peace. It is said that Hera finally made friends with him and that Hercules married one of Hera's daughters. And there he lived in happiness, forever, among the gods.

Nova stars are stars that suddenly increase in brightness and then return to normal. Shown here is Nova Hercules, as seen March 10, 1935, after it brightened as a nova (top), then again two months later on May 6 (bottom) after it had returned to normal. LICK OBSERVATORY.

Again, Hercules is a faint constellation and hard to find. It is hard to find even though you know where to look for it and have seen it before. Because he is so faint, he has been called the Phantom. And because he is shown in a kneeling position he has been called the Kneeling One, and the Kneeler. One poet wrote of Hercules:

Conscious of his shame
A Constellation kneels without a name.

In the early days of Greek history before the constellation had been given a name, although the constellation itself was well-known, it was called the Leaper, and the Keen-eyed One. The Arabs knew him as *Al Rakis*, "the Dancer." There are no outstanding stars in Hercules, at least not to the naked eye. The brightest star in this constellation is the pale yellow star Korneforos (mag. 2.8). The second brightest star in the constellation, the one forming Hercules' head, is known as *Ras Algethi*, from the Arabic meaning "the Kneeler's Head." It is a double star of magnitude of 3.1, one component orange-red and the other bluish-green. Both of its component stars are variable stars. But again, don't expect too much out of this constellation except a whopping good story.

Hercules is best seen from May through October.

CORONA BOREALIS ☆☆☆☆☆☆☆☆☆☆☆☆☆☆☆☆☆☆☆☆☆
(the Northern Crown; also the Northern Cross)

Like Lyra, this is another small constellation with several bright stars, as befitting a royal crown. The crown is located midway between Hercules and Boötes, and the constellation looks very much like a crown.

According to a Greek myth going back to about 450 B.C., a young man named Theseus, son of the king of Athens, touched off the chain of events that led to the Corona Borealis. At this time the ruler of the Island of Crete, King Minos, was so powerful that he was able to demand and get whatever he wished from the people of Athens. Now it happened that Minos kept on Crete a fierce monster called the Minotaur, a beast that was half-bull and

CORONA BOREALIS
(the Northern Crown)

Nusakan

Alphecca

half-man and fed on human flesh. The monster lived in a maze that was so complex that once in it no one could find the way out without help.

Once each year, Minos demanded that the king of Athens send him the seven most handsome young men and the seven most beautiful maidens of the land. These fourteen youths were then forced into the maze where one by one they were found and devoured by the Minotaur.

When Theseus became of age he told his father that he wanted to be one of the youths to be sent to King Minos so that he might slay the Minotaur and once and for all end this terrible reparation

the Athenians had to pay each year. Although he feared that his son would never return, Theseus's father granted the young man his wish.

On the appointed day the fourteen youths boarded the ship to Crete, a ship that always flew black sails, a sign of the certain death awaiting its passengers. When they arrived the youths were paraded before King Minos for him to judge whether all were fair enough for the Minotaur. When the King's daughter, Ariadne, saw Theseus, she immediately fell in love with him and managed to see him alone before the youths were led off to the maze. She told him of her love and gave him a small sword and a ball of thread.

As Theseus led the way into the maze he carefully unwound the ball of thread step-by-step. Eventually he heard the ferocious roars of the Minotaur as it came charging around a corner of the maze to attack him. Theseus dropped the ball of thread and began slashing at the beast with the sword of Ariadne. He managed to weaken the Minotaur and then cut off its head. He then picked up the thread and followed it out of the maze, on the way leading his thirteen companions to safety also.

Now King Minos's guards were taken completely by surprise and after a brief battle all the youths escaped, Ariadne with them. On their way home their ship stopped at the island of Naxos to take on fresh water and Theseus and Ariadne chose to sleep by the shore. In the middle of the night Theseus received a message in a dream from the goddess Minerva telling him that Ariadne had been promised to a god and that no mortal should interfere. So Theseus silently crept away from his bride-to-be, returned to the ship, and ordered that sail be set at once.

When Ariadne awoke next morning and found herself abandoned she wept. As she wept the god Bacchus came upon her and seeing her great beauty begged her to marry him. She said that she could not and furthermore did not believe that he was a god. Whereupon Bacchus produced the most beautiful golden crown she had ever seen, all set with sparkling jewels. Ariadne did marry Bacchus and they had a long life of happiness together.

When his beloved wife, Ariadne, died, Bacchus placed the golden crown high in the heavens to honor her for her kindness to Theseus and to him as her husband.

> Still her sign is seen in heaven,
> And midst the glittering symbols of the sky
> The starry crown of Ariadne glides.

Because this constellation is so bright and easy to find, it is not surprising that several different cultures have myths explaining how it came to be. According to Shawnee Indian legend, twelve beautiful maidens who inhabited the stars of the Northern Crown nightly descended on Earth and danced in the fields. Algon, a Shawnee hunter and handsome youth, chanced to see the maidens one night and fell in love with the youngest of them. Night after night he watched them dance but realized that if he approached them he would frighten them away.

Now Algon had certain magical powers and one night took the form of a field mouse and waited where the maidens danced. As the youngest one approached him, he reappeared as himself and held her tightly. The others fled back up into the sky. When the frightened star-maiden saw what a handsome youth her captor was, she fell in love with him and they were married. But like all star-people, Algon's wife could not forever remain on Earth with mortals. So, in deep sadness, one night she returned to her home in the sky.

Now when the star people saw how sad Algon's wife was they took pity on her, and on Algon and their son. All three were reunited in the sky and forever became associated with the white falcon. In this way they belong to neither sky nor Earth but are free to visit either place whenever it suits them.

To this day we can see the home in the sky of the eleven maidens as that half crown we call the Northern Crown, or as the Shawnee call it, the Celestial Sisters. It is said that the crown is not a complete circle of stars because the youngest maiden is not there with her sisters.

The early Arabs knew the constellation as the Dish, and as the Broken Platter, because it forms an incomplete circle. The ancient Chinese called the constellation *Kwan Soo,* meaning "a Cord." The Australians recognize the constellation as *Woomera,* or "the Boomerang." The brightest star in the Northern Crown is the white star Alphecca (magnitude of 2.2), found at the bottom just off center to the right. Its name is from the Arabic and means "the Bright One of the Dish." It is also sometimes known as Gema and as the Pearl of the Crown. The second brightest star in this constellation is Nusakan (mag. 4).

The Northern Crown is best seen from April through August.

OPHIUCHUS *(the Serpent-Holder)* ☆☆☆☆☆☆☆☆☆☆☆☆☆
SERPENS *(the Serpent)* ☆☆☆☆☆☆☆☆☆☆☆☆☆☆☆☆☆☆☆

These two constellations are considered together because they can be seen as a single constellation once you have had some practice finding it.

There are no especially bright stars in Ophiuchus, although you should not have too much trouble finding the star marking Ophiuchus's head, and

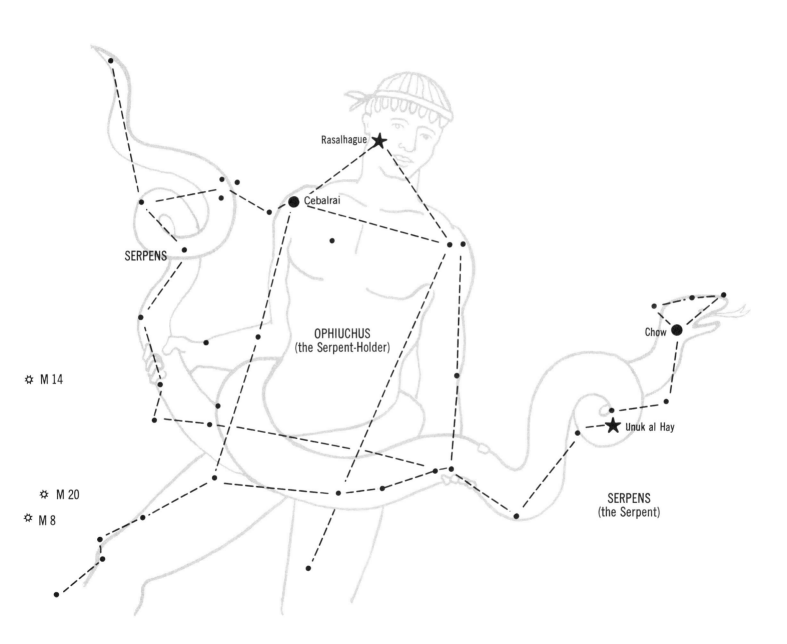

Rasalhague

Cebalrai

SERPENS

OPHIUCHUS
(the Serpent-Holder)

✿ M 14

✿ M 20

✿ M 8

Chow

Unuk al Hay

SERPENS
(the Serpent)

below, the two pairs of stars that mark his shoulders. A fairly straight line of three stars marks his right arm, and another line of about five stars marks his right leg. To the right of Ophiuchus's head is a triangle of stars marking the head of the serpent. Then with some practice you should be able to trace the long winding trail of stars marking the twisting body of the serpent, which Ophiuchus firmly holds in both hands.

If you are good at finding Hercules, just remember that the heads of these two powerful men are side by side, Hercules being seen in the upside down position. It is interesting that both figures represent the powers of light conquering the powers of darkness, in the one case a giant dragon (Draco) and in the other a giant serpent. Both constellations are very old and almost certainly go back to Babylonian and Sumerian mythology when Marduk defeated the powers of darkness represented by the monster Ti'amat (see page 36).

Ophiuchus is a word coming from two Greek words meaning "serpent," and "holding." Ophiu-chus probably was not the actual name of the constellation in early Greek times. Instead it most likely was a term to describe the star group. In the same way, that famous building whose name is the Empire State Building is described more generally as a "skyscraper." The name of the constellation seems to have been identified with the god Aesculapius, expert in the arts of medicine, plants, and the healing powers of different herbs.

Aesculapius, we are told, was the first doctor of medicine, and his expertise led to his downfall in a very strange way. His career seems to have begun when one day while visiting a friend he saw a snake in the room and killed it. Then, to the great surprise of both, a second snake carrying an herb in its mouth crawled into the room. It gave the herb to the first snake, which immediately recovered. It was this herb, which Aesculapius took from the revived snake, that taught him the great powers certain herbs have over life and death. He traveled far and wide over the land, always learning more about the medicinal uses of herbs, and before long his reputation as a saver of lives had become widely known. So expert had he become that Hades, God of the Underworld, complained to his brother Zeus that fewer and fewer souls were being sent down to the Underworld. Hades, of course, was worried about losing his important position.

Aesculapius once is said to have brought Hippolytus back to life by "gluing" him together. Hippolytus (about whom we will have more to say later) had been dragged to death and dismembered when his horses were frightened by a bull. Just as Aesculapius was about to bring the famous giant, Orion, back to life after he had been accidentally shot with an arrow by his lover, Hades' patience ran out. He demanded that Zeus stop this wholesale restoring of life. After all, only the gods were immortal. If Aesculapius were permitted to increase his skill in bringing the dead back to life, mankind, too, would have attained immortality. Thus went Hades' argument to Zeus.

Zeus agreed with his brother and hurled a thunderbolt at Aesculapius, killing him on the spot. But Zeus could not help but admire the skill of Aesculapius and so raised him among the stars as Ophiuchus, along with the serpent from which he had learned his skills.

Aesculapius, as the God of Medicine, is always shown with a staff with a serpent wound around it. You have seen the symbol in hospitals and doctors' offices. Our words *hygiene* (meaning "the science of health") and *panacea* (meaning "a cure-all medicine") come from the names of two of Aesculapius's daughters, Hygeia and Panacea.

Ophiuchus has been known by many other names—the Serpent-Charmer, by the Romans, and the Serpent-Collector, by the Arabs. During the Christian era churchmen tried to change the figure to that of Saint Paul with the Maltese Viper, and another time to Saint Benedict.

This constellation has been the scene of a number of nova stars, or stars that suddenly flare up into brightness for several days or weeks and then return to their former dimness. The first such nova was reported by the Greek astronomer Hipparchos in 134 B.C.; the second in A.D. 123; the third in the year 1230; the one called Kepler's Star in 1604; and the fourth in 1848.

The brightest star in Ophiuchus is the sapphire-colored one forming his head and is known as Rasalhague (magnitude 2.1), from the Arabic *Ras al Hawwa*, meaning "Head of the Serpent Charmer." In China this star is called *How*, or "the Duke." The second brightest star in this constellation is Cebalrai (mag. 2.8), a pale yellow star.

Ophiuchus and Serpens are best seen from July through August.

SCORPIUS (the Scorpion) ☆☆☆☆☆☆☆☆☆☆☆☆☆☆☆☆☆☆

We could write many pages about the evil represented by Scorpius, one of the constellations of the Zodiac. It is one of many monsters of the sky, a leftover demon created by Ti'amat in her battle against the Sun-god Marduk. Scorpius represents death, darkness, and everything that we look on as evil.

As evil as Scorpius may be in mythology and in the charts of the astrologers, he is one of the most splendid constellations in the sky and the most magnificent member of the Zodiac. He is also one of the easiest constellations to find in the sky, with his great sweeping and curving tail at the end of which is a star representing the sting-button of a real scorpion.

Scorpius does not take up much space among the pages of Greek mythology, although he is well represented in the legends of several other lands. The giant hunter, Orion, about whom we will have more to say in the section dealing with the winter constellations, met his fate by the sting of the giant scorpion. While on a hunting expedition with Artemis, Goddess of Wild Animals, Orion boasted that so great was his might and skill as a hunter that he could kill all the animals on the face of Earth. Artemis was alarmed at such a boastful and inappropriate statement, as was Gaea, Goddess of Earth.

After considering what a sad and lonely place Earth would be without all of its many kinds of animals, Gaea decided that Orion must be killed just in case he might one day decide to carry out his boast. So Gaea sent a giant scorpion to Orion and ordered the beast to sting Orion. As mighty as Orion was, after only a brief battle, the scorpion managed to deliver the hunter a deadly sting. Both Orion and the scorpion were given honored places in the sky, but they were placed at opposite ends of the great sky dome so that they would never engage in battle again. Although there are other stories about how Orion met his death, this one is the most common. (For more about Orion, see page 121.)

This constellation is best seen from the Southern Hemisphere, where it dominates the sky almost directly overhead. So it is not surprising to find legends about it from several South Pacific cultures. In New Zealand, for example, the constellation is not regarded as a scorpion, but as a heavenly fishhook. According to one New Zealand myth, a young man by the name of Maui was given a magic jawbone by a goddess of the Underworld. He decided to use the bone as a large fishhook in hopes of catching a very large fish.

He rowed far out to sea. Then after fishing for what seemed a very long time, he realized that he

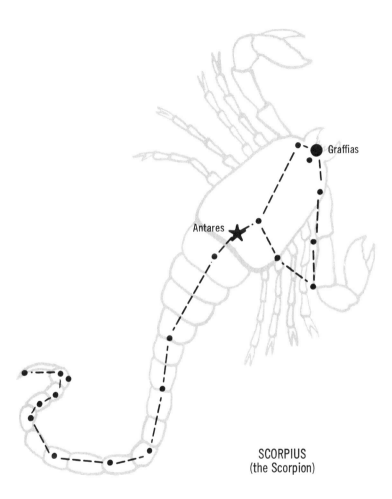

SCORPIUS
(the Scorpion)

Graffias

Antares

had caught something. He had to pull very hard to move the great weight at the end of his line. Whatever it was it did not fight, but just let itself be pulled up and up and up.

When Maui's catch came near enough to the surface so that he could see it in the dim underwater light, he was surprised to find that he had caught an island! There were houses, people walking around or sitting by fires, and dogs and children running along paths in the woods. And that is how the island of New Zealand was formed and came to be called *Te-Ika-a-Maui*, meaning "the Fish of Maui."

So pleased was Maui with his catch, and so grateful was he to the goddess who had given him the magic fishhook, that with all his might he flung the jawbone high into the sky where it became the constellation we today recognize as Scorpius, or the Fish of Maui.

The bright red supergiant star, Antares, has been important in giving Scorpius its evil character. The star forms the Scorpion's heart. The red planet Mars, the Roman God of War, also has been regarded as an evil "star" through history. Just ask any astrologer! The Greek name for Mars is Ares, and *Ant*-ares means the "rival of Mars," or the "equal of Mars." And so it is. When the planet Mars and Antares are both visible in the evening sky, their red fires equal each other, or rival each other, for our attention.

The ancients believed that the red planet Mars was forged from the fires of Antares. They further believed that whenever any planet was seen to pass through Scorpius, dreadful things would occur on Earth. If "your planet" happened to be passing through Scorpius the moment you were born, watch out!

When you compare Antares and Mars remember that Mars is but a planet smaller than Earth while Antares is a supergiant star with a diameter 400 times that of the Sun. They appear to rival each other in brightness only because Mars is so close to us and Antares so very far away (Mars being a mean distance of 228 million kilometers, Antares being approximately 520 light-years away).

The Mayas of Middle America named Scorpius "the Sign of the Death-god." The Romans at one time called it "the Lurking One." The ancient peoples of Asia called the evil Antares "the Grave Digger of Caravans." But the ancient Chinese looked on Antares as a star to be worshiped as a safeguard against fire. They named it *Huo Shing,* meaning "the Fire Star."

While Antares is the brightest star in Scorpius (magnitude of 0.9), the second brightest star is the white star Graffias (mag. 2.7), actually a triple star found in the head of Scorpius. Graffias comes from the Greek and means "crab," which in ancient Greek also meant "scorpion," since these two animals were then thought to be different forms of the same animal. So this may be where our present name for the constellation comes from. Look for Scorpius down near the horizon since it never climbs very high in the sky as seen from northern latitudes. And don't overlook the close pair of stars forming the very tip of the scorpion's tail. The

Arabians called the brighter of these two stars *Shaula,* or "the Sting."

Scorpius is best seen during July and August.

LIBRA (the Scales) ☆☆☆☆☆☆☆☆☆☆☆☆☆☆☆☆☆☆☆☆☆☆☆☆☆

This constellation is located to the right of Scorpius with the constellation Virgo on its right. The ancient Greeks did not recognize Libra. Instead they saw it as part of Scorpius. Evidence for this comes from the names of the two brightest stars in Libra, the Northern Claw and the Southern Claw. It was the Romans who later gave Libra an identity of its own and, therefore, importance as a constellation of the Zodiac.

One of its earliest appearances was that of "the Scales of Justice" held by Julius Caesar. But later the scales became associated with Virgo, the virgin Goddess of Justice. Today we usually represent the constellation simply as "the Scales of Justice" with no one holding them.

While on the subject of inanimate objects, notice that Libra is the first constellation we have dealt with so far that is not an animal of some sort. And it is the only constellation in the twelve making up the Zodiac that is not a living being. Astrologers of the fourteenth century looked on Libra's area of the Zodiac as an evil place, saying:

> *Whoso es born in yat syne sal be an*
> *ill doer and a traytor.*

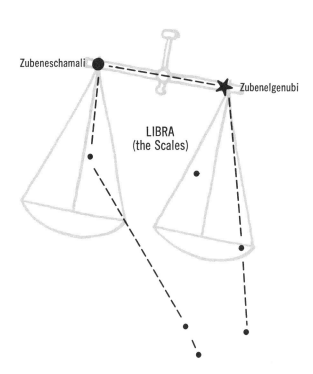

LIBRA
(the Scales)

Zubeneschamali

Zubenelgenubi

Whatever meaning this little constellation might have had in Babylonian times, it has been lost to us. So its significance as a constellation lies not in whatever mythology once might have been attached to it, but in its usefulness. It so happens that in ancient times when the Sun passed through Libra as it crossed the Celestial Equator it marked autumnal equinox, the time of equal day and equal night (about September 22). Now a days, however, the Sun is "in" Libra from October 29 to November 21. This seems a more practical use of the scales, which showed the "weight" of day and night being equal when the Sun occupied this spot in the sky.

> Then Day and Night are weigh'd in Libra's Scales
> Equal a while . . .

The Egyptians also saw in Libra a set of scales, one in which the human heart was to be weighed after death—again, scales of justice. The sacred books of India call this constellation *Tula,* meaning "a balance," and show a man bent on one knee, holding the scales aloft. The ancient Chinese called the constellation *Show Sing,* "the Star of Longevity," but later generations changed the name to *Tien Ching,* meaning "the Celestial Balance." And the appearance of the constellation at a certain time each year marked the time when the annual regulation of weights had to be made by Chinese law.

The two brightest stars in Libra are Zubenelgenubi (magnitude of 2.8), from the Arabic meaning "the Southern Claw" (of Scorpius) and Zubeneschamali (mag. 2.6), meaning "the Northern Claw." The first is actually a widely double star, one component being pale yellow and the other being light gray. The Northern Claw star is a fairly bright star, pale emerald in color.

The best time to observe Libra is during June and July.

SAGITTARIUS (the Archer) ☆☆☆☆☆☆☆☆☆☆☆☆☆☆☆☆☆☆

If Scorpius flicked his tail straight out it would send the stars of Sagittarius flying off in all direc-

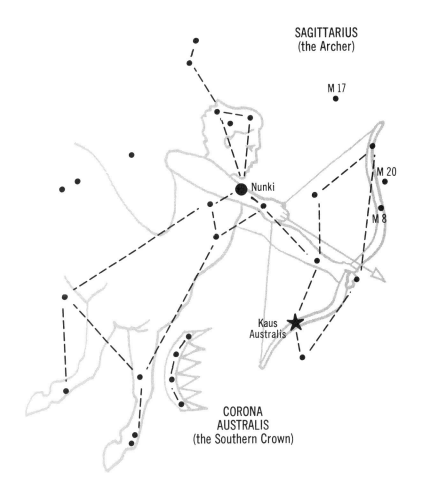

tions. If that helps you remember where Sagittarius, the Archer, is, fine. Another way to remember the position of this Zodiac constellation is to picture Sagittarius poised to shoot an arrow through the heart-star of the Scorpion.

Actually, there is little to mark this constellation except a small arc of five stars that can be seen as a curved bow, and a small upside-down dipper that forms the head of this constellation figure. For the rest of him there are a half dozen or so stars scattered in no particular pattern, but supposedly representing a figure half-man and half-horse.

These creatures were the famed centaurs of Greek mythology. They were rude, untrustworthy, cheating, violent, deceptive, and they drank too much—in all, creatures to be avoided and hardly worth inviting to dinner, that is, all except the one centaur named Chiron. Now Chiron was educated by the Sun-god Apollo and Diana, Goddess of the Moon and of Wild Things. Chiron was as kind, gentle, and wise as the other centaurs were mean, fierce, and unthinking. Chiron's many skills and wisdom became so widely known that children of many a

famous king were sent to him to be taught all manner of skills. Among his pupils were the mighty Hercules and Aesculapius, who became so skilled at medicine (see page 80). And there were others.

One day when Hercules was carrying out one of his twelve labors, he stopped at the house of a friend, the Centaur Pholus. Since Hercules had traveled far that day and was very thirsty he asked Pholus to open a jar of the excellent wine kept in his house but belonging jointly to all the centaurs. Pholus did, and when the aroma of this fine wine flowed out over the countryside the other centaurs furiously galloped up to Pholus's house and demanded to know how he had dared open the wine without first consulting them.

Before poor Pholus could explain matters the other centaurs began to attack him and Hercules. This was a mistake, for Hercules soon settled matters by killing many of them and driving the rest from the country, telling them never to return. One of those so driven away was the centaur Nessus, who was later to be responsible for the death of Hercules. Now it happened that Chiron was nearby observing the event, although he had not taken part and disapproved of the other centaurs' action. Although Hercules knew Chiron, and deeply respected him, he could not recognize his friend from a great distance and accidentally shot him with one of his poisoned arrows. (The arrow had been dipped in the blood of the monster Hydra which Hercules had killed in carrying out one of his labors; see page 64.)

Now Chiron was immortal and could not die. When the poison took effect it pained him so much that he was nearly mad. He pleaded with Zeus to take from him his immortality and permit him to die as a mortal, even though his soul would go down to the Underworld rather than to the home of the gods on Mount Olympus. Zeus took pity on Chiron and granted him his wish. He also gave the good centaur a resting place among the stars as the constellation Sagittarius, the Archer.

There are other versions of this myth but there is no need to include them here.

Sagittarius has been called by many names over the centuries—the Arrow, On Horseback, Horn-footed, and Half-Man among them. The Babylonians, Turks, Persians, and Hebrews all had names for him meaning the Bow. The ancient Egyptians showed the constellation at one time or another as an ibis, a swan, and an archer with a lion's face. The ancient Greeks apparently gave the constellation neither name nor title, although it is recorded in much earlier Babylonian times, sometimes referred to as the Strong One, the Giant King of War, and as the Illuminator of the Great City.

The brightest star in Sagittarius is straight down from the Archer's right shoulder at the upper right foreleg and is known as Kaus Australis (mag. 1.8). Two stars compete for second brightest status, one is Nunki (mag. 1.1) which forms the middle of the archer's head. The other is a double star forming the archer's right shoulder (mag. 2.6). The star Arkab (mag. 3.8 and 8.0), forms the bottom of the left front hoof. This star appears especially bright because it is a double star. As you explore Sagittarius try to spot the three nebulae mentioned earlier, M 20, M 8, and M 17.

Sagittarius is best seen during July and August.

The "Omega" Nebula (M 17, or NGC 6618) in Sagittarius, as photographed through the 200-inch telescope. See constellation diagram and summer star chart for location. HALE OBSERVATORIES.

CORONA AUSTRALIS (*the Southern Crown*) ☆☆☆☆

Right in front of Sagittarius's chest is a little semicircle of four stars forming the Southern Crown. This tiny constellation has been recognized over the centuries by many cultures and has been known by an equal number of different names. It has been called the Southern Wreath by the Greeks. The Romans knew it as the Golden Crown of Sagittarius, as the Little Crown, the Southern Coil, and the Crown of Eternal Life. The Arabs have called it the Tortoise, the Woman's Tent, the Ostrich's Nest, and the Dish (which they also called the Northern Crown). The Chinese also called it the Tortoise, or *Pee*.

AQUILA (*the Eagle*) ☆☆☆☆☆☆☆☆☆☆☆☆☆☆☆☆☆☆☆☆☆☆☆☆☆☆☆

Just above Sagittarius and below Cygnus is a medium-sized constellation called Aquila. Perhaps its main claim to fame is its one bright star, Altair, which is one of the three making up the Summer Triangle. Even though Aquila is not a particularly bright constellation, there are many myths associated with it, both from ancient Greece and the Orient.

It is said in the old Greek myths that during the ten-year war between the followers of Zeus and the Giants a magnificent eagle, known to us as Aquila, was ever by the side of Zeus waiting to carry his

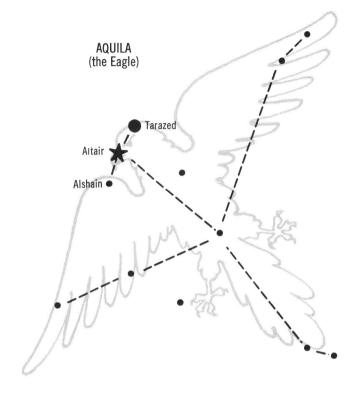

AQUILA
(the Eagle)

Tarazed

Altair

Alshain

thunderbolts down to kill the monstrous Giants. It was for his loyalty that the eagle was given a position among the stars as the constellation Aquila.

But Aquila seems to have performed still other duties that earned him his position of immortality among the stars. It is also said that at one time the gods were in need of a new waiter, a cup-bearer to carry fresh nectar to the gods. It was only fitting that such a privileged position be held by the most beautiful youth on Earth. So Zeus summoned his faithful Aquila, saying: "Go down to Earth and sweep your great wings over the land until your jewellike eyes find the most beautiful youth in the land, and then deliver him to the Great Hall of the Gods."

Aquila raised his powerful wings and glided down to Earth. He swept over the entire land, crossing mountains, rivers, seas, and swamps. Then one day he saw a youth tending a flock of sheep on a mountain side, surely the most beautiful youth in the land. The eagle swiftly dropped out of the sky and ever so gently clasped the youth, Ganymede, in its claws. In spite of being tired from its long journey, the eagle sped upward through the sky and carried Ganymede to Zeus. So delighted was Zeus with Aquila's choice of a cup-bearer for the gods that he reserved a place among the stars for Aquila on his death.

An offshoot of this myth further tells us that when Ganymede died (he being a mortal like Aquila), he was also given a favored place among the stars and became the constellation Aquarius. But there is some argument over this.

Aquila is credited with still another deed. The god Hermes, Messenger of the Gods, had fallen in love with the beautiful Aphrodite, the Goddess of Love. But Aphrodite did not like Hermes and refused to see him. Hermes was crushed and went to Zeus and told him of his deep love and that he would die as a mortal if Aphrodite continued to send him away each time he tried to see her.

Zeus told Hermes that his love would soon pass if Hermes waited and if Aphrodite continued to refuse to see him. But Hermes' love for her became stronger. When it became so strong that he could stand it no more, he went back to Zeus and begged that Zeus help him.

Zeus was understanding and turned to his ever-faithful Aquila and commanded the bird to fly to the shores of the sacred river where Aphrodite bathed each day and steal one of her magic slippers always left by the shore. The eagle sped across the sky and instantly returned with one of the love goddess's slippers in its beak. Zeus then gave the slipper to Hermes who was now in a position to force Aphrodite to see him, and she did.

The Chinese, Japanese, and Koreans also have a myth accounting for Aquila. We are told that the Sun-king had a beautiful daughter named Chih Nu. Now Chih Nu wove the most beautiful tapestries in the land. One day while resting from her work she sat by the window and watched the nearby river shimmering in the sunlight. As she gazed dreamily, her view was broken by the passage of her father's young herdsman, Ch'ien Niu, who tended the royal cattle. He was leading two oxen to the water to drink. As the animals drank, the young man looked around and his eyes met those of Chih Nu who had been watching him with much pleasure. The two instantly fell in love and Chih Nu announced to her father that this man must be her husband.

The Sun-king was delighted with his daughter's choice of a husband because he liked and respected Ch'ien Niu for his hard work and the kindness he always showed when tending the animals. Seven days later the marriage took place. It is said that Chih Nu made her own wedding dress, weaving it out of starlight reflected in the water and in drops of dew.

As the years passed, the two were very happy together, never exchanging an angry word or angry thought. In fact, it was their supreme happiness that was their undoing. Chih Nu began to neglect her weaving, which was her duty as the Weaving Goddess of the Sun-king. And Ch'ien Niu began to neglect his herds and let the oxen wander.

The Sun-king spoke gently to the couple and explained that they must return to their duties, that there still would be time enough to spend with each other. Both promised that they would work as before. And for a while they did, but again both began to neglect their duties. Again the Sun-king spoke to them. But the same thing happened, not only once but several times.

One day as the Sun-king saw the couple sitting idly by the riverbank gazing into each others' eyes he became so angry that he vowed to separate them forever. With but a thought he sent Ch'ien Niu to the far side of that great river flowing across the sky (the Milky Way). And in the same thought he made his daughter a prisoner in her own house on this side of the great river. Although the two pleaded with the Sun-king for mercy and promised that they would work just as hard as they had before their marriage, the Sun-king would not change his mind. Now the Sun-king was a just god and told the couple that he would let them see each other once a year on the seventh day of the seventh month, but they would have to find a way of crossing the great sky river.

Being a mortal, Ch'ien Niu had no powers to make such a crossing. But Chih Nu, being a goddess, had magical powers. She commanded all the magpies of the world to gather by the great sky-river on the appointed day each year. They then were to hover in the air and form a bridge across which Chih Nu could walk to meet her husband. In many villages in Japan the people still celebrate the seventh day of the seventh month by attaching colored paper streamers to poles and placing the poles along the streets. Part of the festival is to write poems to the Goddess of Weaving and then toss the poems into a river or the sea. For all the waters of the world eventually flow into the great river in the sky, so the poems eventually reach Chih Nu, or Tanabata, as she is known in Japan.

To this day we can see Ch'ien Niu as the bright star Vega on one side of the Milky Way in the constellation Lyra, and Chih Nu as the bright star Altair in Aquila.

At least as early as 1200 B.C. this constellation was known as the Eagle. Stone carvings of that age showing the constellation have been found. The constellation also has been called the Bird of Zeus and the King of Birds. The Arabs have called it the Flying Eagle, also the Crow or Raven. The Persians called it the Star-striking Falcon and the Flying Vulture while the Turks called it the Hunting Eagle.

Altair (magnitude of 0.8) is the brightest star in this constellation and, with a neighboring star on each side, forms the Eagle's head. This star takes its name from the Arabic name of the constellation, *Al Nasr al Tair*, meaning, "the Flying Eagle." The second brightest star in the constellation is the one to the upper right of Altair and is a pale orange star called Tarazed (mag. 2.7). Notice the variable star almost straight down from Altair. It has a period of about seven days. You will find that at least three other stars in this constellation compete for second brightest status.

Aquila is best observed from July through October.

DELPHINUS (the Dolphin) ☆☆☆☆☆☆☆☆☆☆☆☆☆☆☆☆☆☆

Look just a bit ahead of Aquila and straight down from Cygnus in the summer sky and you will see a small jewel-box of about six stars, four of which form a neat diamond. This tiny gem of a constellation is Delphinus.

The Greeks may have inherited Delphinus from India, where it also was identified with a dolphin (porpoise). A number of different bits and pieces of Greek myths account for the Dolphin's honored

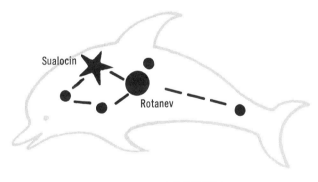

DELPHINUS
(the Dolphin)

place in the sky. According to one, the musician named Arion was the greatest singer who ever existed. (One version of this myth says that he was the greatest harpist.) He was the court musician for the king of Corinth, Periander. So great was Arion's fame that he made a tour of Sicily, having been taken there on a vessel powered by oarsmen.

During his visit to Sicily he was awarded many prizes and given gold and much money. Now the crew of the vessel waiting to take Arion back to Corinth knew of his newly acquired wealth. They plotted to steal it from him and then cast him into the sea sometime during the return voyage. In a dream, Arion was informed by Apollo of the plot against his life. When the time came and the murderous crew made their move, Arion made one last request—that he be permitted to sing a farewell song. The crew could see no danger in that and agreed. So he dressed in his finest court garments and stood in the bow of the ship and began to sing. So sweet was his song that before long sea creatures of many kinds surrounded the ship to listen. Among them was a school of dolphins.

Arion saw that the dolphins seemed very pleased with his song and just before he reached the end of it he plunged overboard amid the dolphins. One of the animals caught him even before he struck the water and raced off with him toward Corinth. It was with great difficulty that Arion hung on, so swift was the dolphin's course through the sea. The startled crew looked on helplessly and believed that surely Arion would fall off the dolphin and drown.

But the dolphin safely carried Arion to Corinth, whereupon Arion made his way home to the court of King Periander. Now the king was happy to see Arion again and listened to his story with much interest, but he found it difficult to believe. "Wait until the vessel arrives home," Arion said, "and see what story the crew has to tell."

When the vessel docked, Periander met it while Arion hid from sight. The crew said that Arion had decided to remain in Sicily, so great was the wealth he had acquired there. At that moment Arion stepped into view and the crew were so terrified that they confessed their plot. King Periander crucified them to the last man. So pleased was Apollo with the good dolphin's role in rescuing Arion that the god gave the dolphin a place among the stars.

At one time the Arabs called the constellation *Al Ka'ud,* "the Riding Camel." The early Christians saw it as the Cross of Jesus. The four brightest stars of the constellation have also been called the Pearls, or Precious Stones. For many centuries after about A.D. 150, the stars of this constellation were regarded by astrologers as especially important ones involving human births and character.

The brightest star in this constellation is Sualocin (magnitude of 4) and is pale yellow. The second brightest star, Rotanev, is a double star (mags. 4 and 6) greenish in color. For a long while the names of these two stars were a puzzle. It turned out, however, that when considered together and spelled backward the names spelled Nicolaus Venator, the Latin name of the Italian astronomer Niccolo Cacciatore, of Piazzi.

Delphinus is best observed July through November.

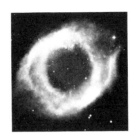

The Autumn Sky

The autumn sky is not as crowded with constellations as the summer sky is, but there is still a lot to see. Some of our summer friends are still with us, all of Delphinus and part of Cygnus, with its bright star Deneb, for example.

Pegasus, the Winged-Horse, is in full view this time of the year and spreads himself over a large part of the sky. Four bright stars mark his Great Square. Andromeda also is clearly seen during this season. Here you will be able to see M 31, the Andromeda Galaxy, one of the most splendid galaxies visible to us. You can see this object with the unaided eye as a tiny fuzzy patch. Binoculars will enlarge it considerably, and a small telescope even more. M 31 is a spiral galaxy, like our own, but twice as large and lying some two million light-years away. But as galaxies go, Andromeda is a fairly close neighbor.

Just beneath the Great Square of Pegasus is one of the fishes forming the constellation Pisces, the Fishes. And just beneath Pisces is Cetus, the Whale, fully visible this time of the year. Perseus,

The famous Andromeda Galaxy (M 31, or NGC 224) in Andromeda as seen through the 48-inch Schmidt telescope. This galaxy is visible to the naked eye. It is similar to our own and about the same size. The two bright spots are satellite galaxies of Andromeda's. HALE OBSERVATORIES.

An open spiral galaxy (M 33, or NGC 598) near Triangulum and Pisces as seen through the 200-inch telescope. See constellation diagram (page 107) and autumn star chart (next page) for location. HALE OBSERVATORIES.

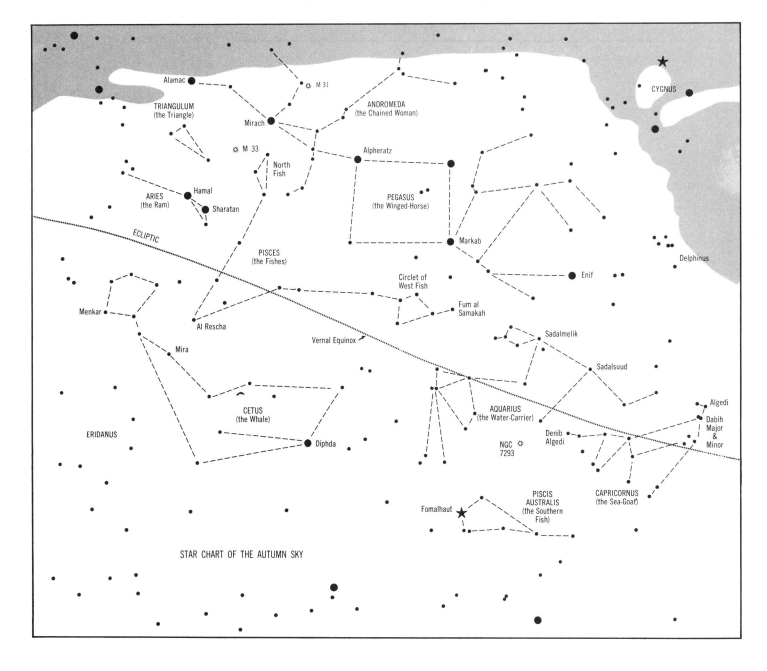

STAR CHART OF THE AUTUMN SKY

the Whale's slayer, is only partly visible in the northeastern part of the sky. Just above the tail of Cetus is Aries, the Ram. To the northwest of Aries is M 33, another spectacular spiral galaxy. To the right of Cetus is the constellation Aquarius, the Water-Carrier. And just to the right of Aquarius is most of the constellation Capricornus, the Sea-Goat. Then below and to the left of Capricornus is a small constellation, Piscis Australis, the Southern Fish. There is a particularly bright star called Fomalhaut in this constellation. Try to find it.

A rather interesting star in the autumn sky is

The autumn star chart shows only those constellation figures mentioned in the text, although numerous additional stars are shown. All star-shaped stars represent stars of magnitude 1.5 and brighter. The large-dot stars represent stars of magnitude 2 to 2.5. The small-dot stars represent stars with magnitudes less than 2.5. Note the long broken line representing the ecliptic. Expect to find planets along and near this ecliptic-line. The light shaded area represents the Milky Way.

Mira, in Cetus. Mira is a "disappearing" star. It is a red variable star with a period of a little less than a year. When at full brightness it is brilliant, but when most dim it cannot be seen even with binoculars.

ANDROMEDA (the Chained-Woman) ☆☆☆☆☆☆☆☆☆☆

We told the myth involving the family of Andromeda on page 39). She was the young woman chained to the rocks along the sea coast and left to be devoured by the sea-monster Cetus in order to appease the anger of Poseidon, God of the Sea. However, Perseus, part of whom we can see this season beside Andromeda in the northeast sky, rescued her and married her.

The brightest star in Andromeda is Alpheratz (magnitude of 2.1), from the Arabic *Al Surrat al Faras*, which means "the Horse's Navel." At one time the Arabs associated Alpheratz with the Winged-Horse, of which Alpheratz forms the top left corner. Andromeda is seen pretty much standing on her head, and Alpheratz is the head-star. The

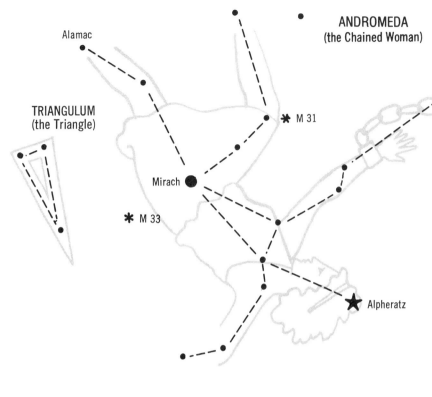

star, by the way, is a white double star with a very dim purplish companion. If Alpheratz happens to be your star, the astrologers tell us, you may expect to be heaped with honors and riches. If you were born at 9:00 p.m., November 10, you can claim Alpheratz as your star. The second brightest star in this constellation is the yellow Mirach (mag. 2.0). It marks the right side of Andromeda. Be sure to locate M 31 in this constellation.

Andromeda is best observed from September through January.

TRIANGULUM (the Triangle) ☆☆☆☆☆☆☆☆☆☆☆☆☆☆☆

This is a small and rather faint constellation just beneath Andromeda's right foot and just above Aries. It is an old constellation and is said to represent the island of Sicily, having been honored by Zeus with an eternal position among the stars. One of its early names was Sicilia. It was in this constellation that the Italian astronomer Giuseppe Piazzi discovered the first asteroid, Ceres, on New Year's Day, 1801. Try to locate M 33 in this constellation.

Triangulum is best seen from about October through February.

ARIES (the Ram) ☆☆☆☆☆☆☆☆☆☆☆☆☆☆☆☆☆☆☆☆☆☆☆☆☆

Athamas, King of Orchomenus, had taken a new wife, Ino. Now Ino was a jealous woman and was extremely envious of Phrixus and his sister Helle, Athamas's two children by his first wife. After much persuasion by Ino, Athamas agreed to sacrifice his son, Phrixus, who would have inherited his father's kingdom. Now the god Hermes was aware of the death plot against the boy and at the last minute sent down from heaven a beautiful and powerful ram with golden fleece.

Phrixus and Helle both climbed onto the ram's back and were carried off through the air. Poor Helle was unable to hang on and fell to her death over the strait named after her, the Hellespont, which links the Aegean Sea with the Sea of Marmara in what is now Turkey. Phrixus managed to hang on and was carried by Aries to a land near the Black Sea called Colchis, the capital of which

was Aea. Because the young man had been brought to Aea by the gods, Phrixus was welcomed by its king, Aeetes.

Now that the golden ram's work was done, the ram commanded Phrixus to sacrifice him to the gods and remove his golden fleece. Phrixus did and presented the golden fleece to **King Aeetes**, who

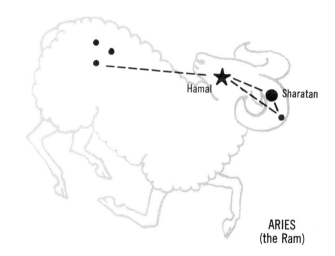

ARIES
(the Ram)

was delighted with the gift. The King hung the fleece in the sacred Grove of Ares, where there lived a dragon who never slept and guarded the golden fleece. We are told that so brilliantly did the golden fleece shine that by night it bathed the surrounding countryside in a warm golden light. The brave and generous ram was given an eternal place in the sky as the constellation Aries. It is said that this constellation is a dim one because at the time the ram was immortalized it no longer had its brightly shining fleece.

After observing this constellation you may wonder why the ancients ever bothered grouping such a dim association of stars. It happens that around 1800 B.C. the position occupied by Aries on the Zodiac band was an important one, and will be again in the distant future. It marked the beginning of spring and was known as the First Point of Aries. So in their attempts to keep track of the Sun's month-by-month progress around the Zodiac, the ancients needed a marker of some sort to indicate the beginning of spring. And the only stars occupy-ing that particular place on the Zodiac at that time were those dim ones we now recognize as the constellation Aries.

The ram was an important mythological figure. In Greek mythology it was identified with Zeus. And the Egyptians associated the ram with their Sun-god, Ammon. To this day the astrologers' almanacs list the ram as the "Leader of the Host of the Zodiac."

> The Ram having pass'd the Sea serenely shines,
> And leads the Year, the Prince of all the Signs.

Many different peoples of ancient times knew this constellation as a ram or a sheep. But the Chinese knew it as a dog, *Kiang Leu*. Later they knew it as *Pih Yang*, or "the White Sheep." Early Christians looked on the constellation as the lamb sacrificed on Calvary for the sins of humans. Aries is a dreaded astrological sign, supposedly causing us to be "wicked of temper and bodily hurt." In May of the year 1012 a nova reportedly was seen in this constellation.

The brightest star in Aries is the yellowish Hamal (magnitude of 2.0), from the Arabic *Al Ras al Hamal*, meaning "the Head of the Sheep." As the ancient Egyptians oriented the construction of many of their pyramids in relation to the star Thuban in the constellation Draco, so the Greeks from about 1580 B.C. to 360 B.C. oriented the construction of many of their sacred temples in relation to Hamal. The second brightest star in this constellation is Sharatan (mag. 2.7), a rather dim white star.

The best time to observe Aries is from October through February.

PEGASUS (the Winged-Horse) ☆☆☆☆☆☆☆☆☆☆☆☆☆☆☆☆

The story of Pegasus was told on page 40. After Perseus cut off the head of the serpent-haired Medusa and was carrying the head away, some of the blood dripped into the sea and out of it Poseidon fashioned the Winged-Horse.

The famous Great Square is only part of this constellation. Since it covers such an enormous area

PEGASUS
(the Winged-Horse)

of the sky you may have trouble finding it at first. The Arabs knew this part of the constellation as *Al Dalw*, or "the Water-Bucket." The brightest star in Pegasus is the white star Markab (magnitude of 2.5), Arabian for "saddle," "ship," "vehicle," or anything one can ride on, it seems. It is the bottom right star in the Great Square. The second brightest star in this constellation is Scheat (mag. 2.5), a deep yellow variable star with an irregular period. This star marks the top right corner of the Great Square across from Alpheratz, which forms Andromeda's head.

Pegasus is best seen from August through October.

PISCES (the Fishes) ☆☆☆☆☆☆☆☆☆☆☆☆☆☆☆☆☆☆☆☆☆☆☆☆

This constellation today can claim the importance that Aries commanded for so many centuries. It contains that point in the sky occupied by the Sun during Vernal Equinox, the day on which the hours of daylight and night are equal, which falls about March 21. So Pisces, rather than Aries, can claim the number one position of importance among the twelve constellations of the Zodiac.

Pisces is not an easy constellation to find and it is spread out over a rather large section of the sky.

It might be helpful for you to imagine the constellation as two fishlines joined by a knot, at each end of which hangs a fish. The Northern Fish is formed by a small triangle of stars between the upper left star in the Great Square (Alpheratz) and the star forming the top of the small constellation Triangulum. In fact, the Triangle points nearly directly at the Northern Fish.

To find the Western Fish, follow the fishline down and to the left toward Cetus, the Whale. When you come to the greenish star called Al Rescha, and which forms the knot joining the two fishlines, turn up and to the right to follow the other branch of the line leading to the Western Fish. This fish forms what is called the Circlet, a pentagon of five stars lying right under the Great Square. Pisces is one of three Zodiac constellations associated with the rainy season and sharing a position in the great Sky Sea. When the Sun passes through these three constellations it is a signal for the rainy season to begin. Because they were thought to bring rain when it was most needed, it is not

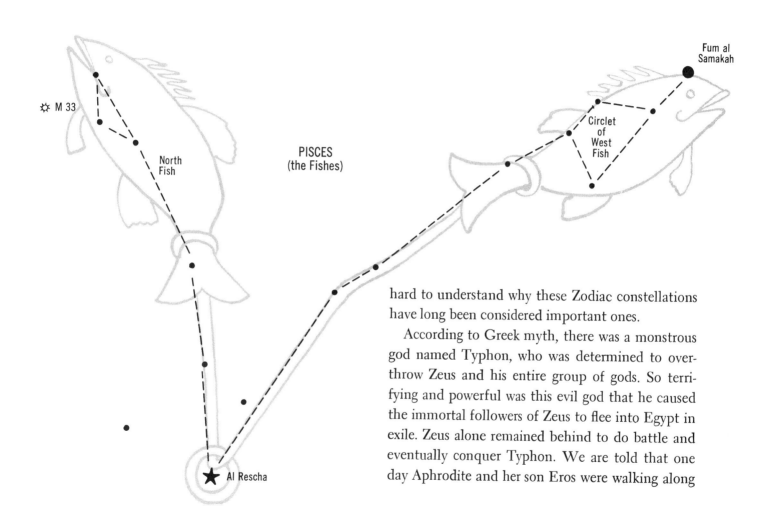

☼ M 33

North
Fish

Fum al
Samakah

Circlet
of
West
Fish

PISCES
(the Fishes)

★ Al Rescha

hard to understand why these Zodiac constellations have long been considered important ones.

According to Greek myth, there was a monstrous god named Typhon, who was determined to overthrow Zeus and his entire group of gods. So terrifying and powerful was this evil god that he caused the immortal followers of Zeus to flee into Egypt in exile. Zeus alone remained behind to do battle and eventually conquer Typhon. We are told that one day Aphrodite and her son Eros were walking along a riverbank when they sensed the presence of the monstrous god Typhon. Quickly they plunged into the river where they took the form of fishes and escaped. To this day we see them as the Northern Fish and the Western Fish of Pisces.

As we might guess, a constellation associated with the arrival of the rainy season, so important to farmers, must have a long history. This constellation was known by the Babylonians as Nunu, by the Persians as Mahik, and by the Turks as Balik, all meaning "Fish." The Chinese, however, called it at various times the Dark Warrior, the Northern Emperor, and the Pig. But after missionaries were established in that country the constellation became known popularly as the Two Fishes. The Arabs also knew it as *Al Samakatain*, or "the Two Fishes." The Syrians regarded fish as holy animals and so refused to eat them. Their divinity is summed up nicely in these lines by the Roman poet Ovid:

Hence Syrians hate to eat those kinds of fishes;
Nor is it fit to make their gods their dishes.

The brightest star in Pisces is a double star called Al Rescha (magnitudes of 4 and 5.5). One component is pale green and the other blue. It is this star that forms the knot joining the two fishlines. The name comes from the Arabic *Al Risha*, meaning "the Cord." The second brightest star listed in the constellation is called by the Arabs *Fum al Samakah* (mag. 4.5), meaning "the Fish's Mouth."

The best time to observe Pisces is from October through January.

CETUS (the Whale) ☆☆☆☆☆☆☆☆☆☆☆☆☆☆☆☆☆☆☆☆☆☆☆☆☆

We met Cetus earlier (page 39) when we told the story of Perseus's daring rescue of Andromeda, the maiden chained by the sea coast waiting to be devoured by the sea-monster sent by Poseidon to ravage the land.

Autumn is the time to observe Cetus in his full glory. He forms a large constellation just below Pisces and to the left of Aquarius. The head of our sea-monster is formed by a pentagon of five stars just under Aries. Its body then stretches down and to the right. It is not surprising to find religious scholars of the late Christian era seeing in Cetus the whale that swallowed Jonah. To the eyes of some, the constellation looks more like a reclining chair than a whale, the whale's head being the headrest of the chair. Cetus is another good example of a "see-it-yourself" constellation.

The brightest star in this constellation is the yellow star Diphda (magnitude of 2.0), also known as Deneb Kaitos. The name comes from the Arabic *Al Dhanab al Kaitos al Janubiyy*, which means "the Tail of the Whale Toward the South," and that's just where the star is found.

The second brightest star in Cetus is the one called Menkar (mag. of 2.5), the left of the two bright stars forming the bottom of Cetus's head. It is from the Arabic *Al Minhar*, meaning "the Nose," although the star actually marks the open jaws of Cetus. Menkar is a bright orange star and to astrologers of old brought danger from large beasts. It also meant disgrace and bad luck to those born under its influence.

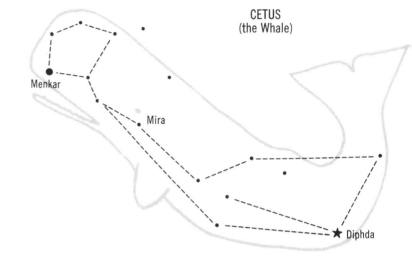

The feature attraction in Cetus is the star Mira, which was mentioned earlier. Called *Stella Mira* by the Romans, and meaning "the Wonderful Star," it is a reddish variable star having a period of somewhat less than a year. Sometimes it grows so dim (mag. 9.5) that it cannot be seen at all. Other times it may remain invisible to the naked eye for several years. When at its brightest (about 2 or less mag.) the star may be 1,500 times brighter than when at its dimmest. It tends to remain at its brightest for about two weeks, taking about seven weeks to get that way. Then it decreases in brightness over a period of about three months. By all means, search for Mira.

The best time to observe Cetus is from October through January.

AQUARIUS (the Water-Carrier) ☆☆☆☆☆☆☆☆☆☆☆☆☆☆

The second of our "water" constellations in the Zodiac is Aquarius. As with Pisces, when the Sun passed through Aquarius, it heralded the rainy season, an extremely important time for all cultures depending on agricultural activities for survival.

You will find Aquarius almost directly beneath the Western Fish in Pisces and to the right of Cetus, the Whale. Like Pisces, Aquarius is an old constellation. As the Water-Carrier he is carved on stones of the Babylonian Empire and probably is still older than that period. In Egyptian mythology he pours water into the River Nile at the season when the Nile normally overflows its banks and brings the much-needed water to the farmlands bordering that great river. The Arabs, also dependent on water of the rainy seasons, adopted Aquarius from an earlier time. But because their religion forbids them from showing pictures of any living form, they show this constellation simply as a water bucket alone.

In ancient Greece, Aquarius was at one time associated with Zeus, as the basic force giving rise to life. In another Greek myth Aquarius is identified with a man and his wife known as Deucalion and Pyrrha. According to the myth, in 1500 B.C. Aquarius (possibly representing Zeus) caused a great flood to wash over Earth. Deucalion's father, Prometheus, advised his son and wife to build a great boat and stock it with provisions. They did and the two floated in the world-sea for nine days and nine nights. Eventually they ran aground on Mount Parnassus.

Safe but lonely, the two sole survivors of Earth walked about as the waters became lower and ex-

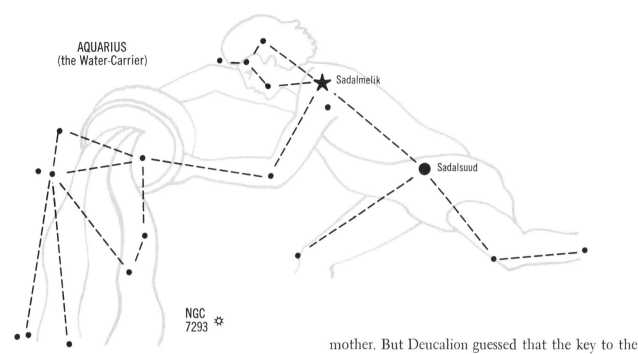

AQUARIUS
(the Water-Carrier)

Sadalmelik

Sadalsuud

NGC
7293 ☼

posed more and more of the land. What were they to do? They appealed to an oracle and were told to ". . . throw over your shoulders the bones of your mother."

"But what does that mean?" Deucalion asked of his wife. Pyrrha did not know either. At first she said that she refused to dig up the bones of her

mother. But Deucalion guessed that the key to the message was different. "The bones of Mother Earth," said Deucalion, "must be stones." So as the two walked along they picked up stones and kept tossing them over their shoulders. After a while they looked behind them and there were people. The stones that Deucalion had thrown had become men, and those thrown by Pyrrha had become women.

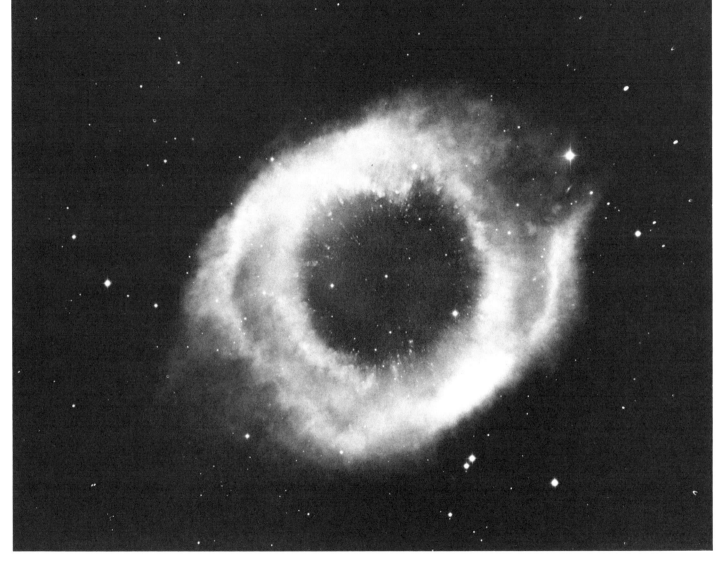

This is a "planetary" nebula in Aquarius (NGC 7293) as seen through the 200-inch telescope. (These nebulae have nothing to do with planets.) See constellation diagram and autumn star chart for location. HALE OBSERVATORIES.

And so the Water-Carrier, in the guise of Zeus, became the taker-away of life and the giver of life. This myth of a world flood and then a rebirth of life on Earth is a common one and can be found in many myths. Our only interest in it here is that the constellation Aquarius is the significant figure in this Greek myth.

Aquarius as the God of the Waters must have been regarded as a good god by some and a bad god by others, depending on the prevailing climate of their region. To the Egyptians, Greeks, and others who lived in lands plagued by a dry climate, Aquarius surely was looked on as a kindly god who brought the rains when they were most needed during the planting season. But in lands plagued with a wet climate he must have been looked on as an evil god. The Babylonians at one time looked on Aquarius as a bad god and referred to the month when the Sun was in Aquarius as the month of "the curse of rain." In both ancient India and China this constellation also was a watery sign.

The brightest star in Aquarius is a pale yellow one just a bit southwest of the circlet forming the Western Fish in Pisces. It is called Sadalmelik (magnitude of 2.9), from the Arabic *Al Sa'd al Malik*, meaning "the Lucky One of the King." The second brightest star in this constellation is also a pale yellow one and is located just a bit southwest of Sadalmelik. It is called Sadalsuud (mag. 2.9), from the Arabic *Al Sa'd al Su'ud*, meaning "the Luckiest of the Lucky." The name comes from the fact that when this star was seen to rise with the Sun, winter had passed and the season of gentle and continuous rain had finally arrived, a time for planting.

The best time to see Aquarius is in October, but it is also visible in September and November.

CAPRICORNUS (the Sea-Goat) ☆☆☆☆☆☆☆☆☆☆☆☆☆☆

Capricornus is another of those dim constellations hard to find and hard to see. Like Aries, its importance is not in its stars or shape, but in the fact that it occupies an important position along the Zodiac. Long ago Winter Solstice occurred in

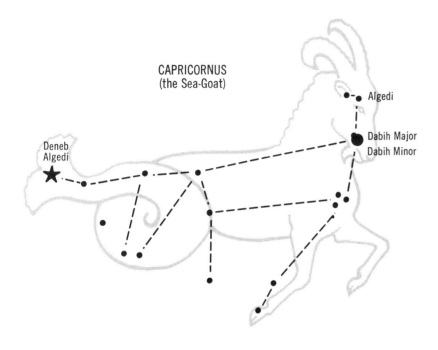

CAPRICORNUS
(the Sea-Goat)

Algedi

Dabih Major
Dabih Minor

Deneb
Algedi

the third Zodiacal watery constellation.

You'll recall from what we had to say about Pisces that at one time the young Greek gods led by Zeus were at battle with the Giants. But when the monster-god Typhon appeared all the young gods except Zeus fled into Egypt, so fearsome was Typhon's appearance.

There is confusion over how Capricornus came to be. Some say that he represents the Shepherd-god Pan. Others say that he was quite a different god, Aegipan. Now so terrible was the sight of Typhon that Zeus himself is said to have changed himself into the form of the ram, Aries, and remained that way for a while. The other gods also changed themselves into animal forms. Aphrodite and Eros, for example, transformed themselves into the two fishes forming the constellation Pisces.

When Zeus reappeared in his own form and prepared to do battle with Typhon, Zeus was defeated. Typhon cut out the tendons of Zeus's hands and feet and so made him helpless to move. He

Capricornus. Winter Solstice marks the shortest day of the year, after which the Sun begins to climb higher in the sky each day and the days grow longer. Winter Solstice now occurs around December 22, but in the constellation Sagittarius. Capricornus is then hid the tendons in a cave in the land of Cilicia. And to guard the tendons he selected the dragon-woman Delphyne, half-serpent and half-woman. Now Delphyne wasn't a very good guard and permitted the tendons to be stolen by the gods Hermes and Aegipan. Earlier, Aegipan, like the other gods, had transformed himself into an animal to escape detection by Typhon. He had jumped into the river when Typhon approached. But he was already halfway submerged before he thought of what form of animal he would wear. He decided to be a goat. So a goat he became, but only from the waist up. From the waist down he took the form of a fish.

Aegipan and Hermes managed to steal the tendons of Zeus and return them, making Zeus once again as fit as ever. His strength regained, Zeus unleashed all his fury and killed the monster Typhon by hurling thunderbolts at him. For Aegipan's role in this battle against the Giants, Zeus gave him an honored place in the sky as the constellation Capricornus.

Capricornus is another constellation whose history we can trace to Babylonian times. And his appearance then was as it is now, half-fish and half-goat. The Arabs, Persians, Turks, and Syrians all knew the constellation as the Goat. In certain parts of the Orient the constellation was known as the Southern Gate of the Sun, indicating that it is in this constellation that the Sun reaches its lowest point on the ecliptic and thereafter begins to appear higher and higher each day.

The brightest star in Capricornus is the one near the end of the animal's tail and is called Algedi (magnitude of 2.9), from the Arabian constellation called *Al Jady*. It is a faint yellow double star. The second brightest star in this constellation is across the constellation in the goat's head. It is actually a pair of double stars called Dabih Major and Dabih Minor (mag. 3.1). Each pair consists of an orange-yellow and sky-blue star.

Capricornus is best seen in August through October.

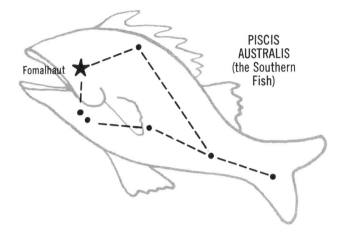

PISCIS
AUSTRALIS
(the Southern
Fish)

Fomalhaut

PISCIS AUSTRALIS (the Southern Fish) ☆☆☆☆☆☆☆☆

This constellation is hardly worth mentioning since it is so low in the sky as seen from mid-latitudes of the Northern Hemisphere. The only reason we might mention it here and show it on our chart is for its very bright star Fomalhaut (magnitude of 1.2), which is one of the fifteen brightest stars seen in our sky.

To find this reddish star just use as "pointers" the two stars forming the righthand edge of the Great Square and imagine a line dropping straight down through Aquarius. And there is Fomalhaut. The star will be visible from about September through November. So if you happen to spot a bright object about where you think Fomalhaut should be in months other than those, you can be sure that it is a planet. Fomalhaut's name comes from the Arabic *Fum al Hut*, meaning "the Fish's Mouth."

The Winter Sky

WHAT TO LOOK FOR ☆☆☆☆☆☆☆☆☆☆☆☆☆☆☆☆☆☆

Since the nights are growing longer now and the stars appearing earlier, the winter sky begins to rival the summer sky for many splendid sky objects. You are bound to be impressed with the large number of very bright stars in the winter sky.

The constellation that dominates winter is the famous Hunter, Orion. He can boast of more bright stars than any other constellation in the sky. Rivaling even Hercules in his might, Orion has two supergiant stars, plus a spectacular nebula (M 42) marking his sword. IC 434, better known as the Horsehead Nebula, also is found in Orion.

You can use Orion to locate several other sky objects. For example, follow the three stars in Orion's belt downward and you will find the bright star Sirius. Follow a line extending eastward through Orion's shoulders and you will find the three bright stars Procyon, Regulus, and Denebola, in that order. Look behind Orion and you will find his two faithful hunting dogs, Canis Major and Canis Minor, following their master.

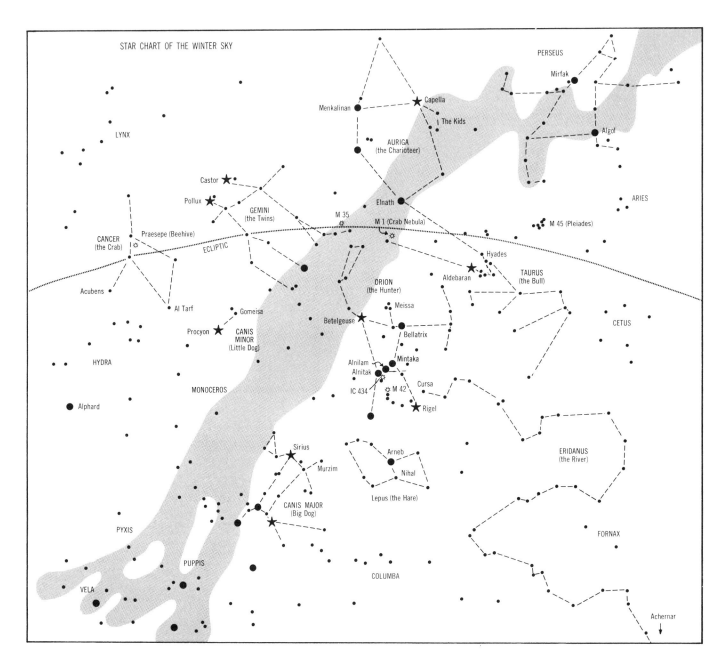

STAR CHART OF THE WINTER SKY

PERSEUS

Mirfak

Capella

Menkalinan

The Kids

Algol

LYNX

AURIGA
(the Charioteer)

ARIES

Castor

Elnath

M 45 (Pleiades)

Pollux

GEMINI
(the Twins)

M 35

M 1 (Crab Nebula)

CANCER
(the Crab)

Praesepe (Beehive)

Hyades

ECLIPTIC

Aldebaran

TAURUS
(the Bull)

Acubens

ORION
(the Hunter)

CETUS

Al Tarf

Gomeisa

Meissa

Procyon

CANIS
MINOR
(Little Dog)

Betelgeuse

Bellatrix

HYDRA

Alnilam
Alnitak

Mintaka

MONOCEROS

Alphard

IC 434

M 42

Cursa

Rigel

ERIDANUS
(the River)

Sirius

Murzim

Arneb

Nihal

Lepus (the Hare)

CANIS MAJOR
(Big Dog)

PYXIS

FORNAX

PUPPIS

COLUMBA

VELA

Achernar

To the north and west of the Hunter is the great Bull, Taurus, offering to one and all two lovely open star clusters—the Hyades and the Pleiades. The bright red star Aldebaran, in Taurus, glares down belligerently at the giant Hunter. Above Taurus is poised the Charioteer, Auriga, with the beautiful, brilliant yellow star Capella just above Orion's head. Binoculars will reveal a number of star clusters in Auriga. Perseus, our hero who rescued the chained Andromeda, is nearly in full view in the winter northern sky. Newcomers to our list are Gemini, the Twins, who occupy a place of importance nearly equaling that of Orion, and whose bright stars Pollux and Castor follow the Hunter closely. The Crab, or Cancer, lies just to the east of

Like the Big Dipper, Orion can be used as a "pointer" constellation to help locate certain stars. Follow the giant's belt down to the left and you will find Sirius. Follow a line through his shoulders and you will find the bright stars Procyon (in Canis Minor), and Regulus and Denebola (both in Leo).

The winter star chart shows only those constellation figures mentioned in the text, although numerous additional stars are shown. All star-shaped stars represent stars of magnitude 1.5 and brighter. The large-dot stars represent stars of magnitude 2 to 2.5. The small-dot stars represent stars with magnitudes less than 2.5. Note the long broken line representing the ecliptic. Expect to find planets along and near this ecliptic-line. The light shaded area represents the Milky Way.

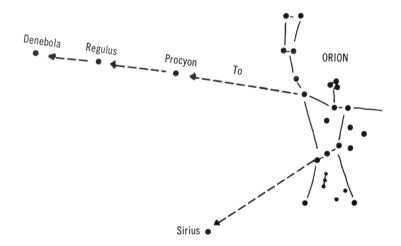

The Great Nebula (M 42, or NGC 1976) in Orion as seen through the 100-inch telescope. See constellation diagram and winter star chart for location. HALE OBSERVATORIES.

The "Horsehead" Nebula (IC 434) in Orion as seen through the 200-inch telescope. See constellation diagram and winter star chart for location. HALE OBSERVATORIES.

Gemini. And in the southern sky you will find the Big Dog, Canis Major, and the Little Dog, Canis Minor. Also there is the great river of the sky, Eridanus, and numerous other interesting sky objects.

ORION (the Hunter) ☆☆☆☆☆☆☆☆☆☆☆☆☆☆☆☆☆☆☆☆☆

Orion was a giant hunter. As far back as we can trace through history he was associated with the forces of goodness and light. He was the Sun-god of both the Egyptians and Phoenicians.

Orion is said to be the son of Poseidon and the mortal Euryale, who was the daughter of King Minos. Orion's first wife was Side, a vain woman who boasted that she was more beautiful even than Hera, the Queen of Heaven. Hera, being a very jealous woman, punished Side by sending her down to Hades.

After losing his wife, Orion voyaged to the island of Chios where he fell in love with Merope, daughter of King Oenopion. Although the king promised Orion his daughter's hand in marriage, he

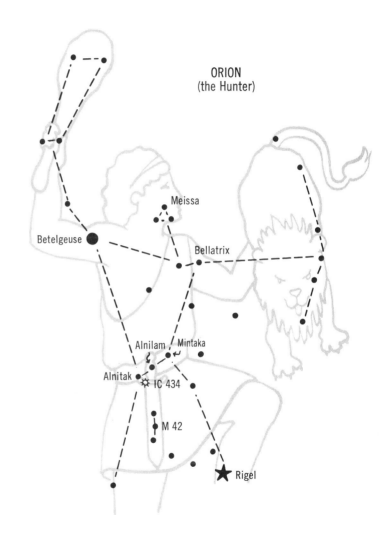

ORION
(the Hunter)

kept delaying the wedding, each time giving Orion a new and difficult task to perform in order for Orion again and again to prove his worthiness. Eventually Orion came to realize that the king's promises meant nothing and that Oenopion really never intended to let his daughter marry him.

In despair, Orion planned to carry Merope away, by force if necessary. Unfortunately the plan was discovered and the King's guards seized Orion and locked him up. Oenopion was furious with himself for having managed things so poorly and took out his rage on Orion by blinding him and casting him onto the beach to fend for himself.

Now because Orion was the son of Poseidon, he had the powers of walking on the surface of the seas. And this he began to do on hearing the ringing of a distant blacksmith's hammer. Following the sound he went to the island of Lemnos and to the artisan-smith Hephaestus who fashioned beautiful ornaments of silver and gold, and armor for the gods. Hephaestus pitied the blind giant and gave Orion one of his servants, Cedalion, as a guide.

Placing Cedalion on his great shoulders, Orion told him to guide them to the east. Orion knew that it was there, in the east, where he could have his sight restored. Eventually they came to the land of the rising Sun, the domain of the Sun-god Apollo. At sunrise the next day Orion faced the Sun and was warmed by its rays. Looking in the direction of the Sun, Orion felt his eyes come alive. First he saw as if through fog, then as clearly as ever before.

With his eyesight regained, the giant made his way to the island of Crete to live. There he hunted game and led a happy life. One day he met Artemis, Goddess of Wild Animals and of the Moon, who also liked to hunt. They fell in love and spent many days together. Now each night Artemis was supposed to drive her silver Moon-chariot across the sky. On noticing that there had been no Moon for several nights, Apollo became angry with his sister and told her that she must not neglect her duties any longer. But so great was her love for the handsome giant that she ignored her brother's words.

Then one day near sunset Apollo tricked his

sister. He had seen Orion bathing by himself by the shore. With his blinding rays, Apollo caused a bright patch of light to surround Orion on the water. Only a dim gray patch in the middle could be seen. Apollo next teased Artemis by saying that she had been spending so much time with her lover that she had lost her eye as a marksman and he challenged her to hit the dark spot in the center of the shimmering patch of light. Artemis was angry with her brother for teasing her and quickly sent an arrow across the sea to its mark, killing her lover.

Later, when Orion's body was washed ashore by the waves, Artemis was horrified to see her arrow and to learn that she had been tricked by Apollo. In great sadness she tenderly placed the body of Orion in her silver Moon-chariot and carried him high up into the sky. Then finding the darkest place, so that his stars would shine the brightest of all surrounding stars, she placed him where we see him today. If you look carefully you can see the giant hunter, club raised, great belt bearing a sword, and carrying a lion's skin for his shield. (For another version of how Orion met his death, see Scorpius, page 82.)

Orion was known in ancient Greece, around 500 B.C., as the Warrior, and in Akkadia as the Light of Heaven. He was also known as the Foot-turning Wanderer (a reference to him during his period of blindness), and as the Madman. The ancient Arabians called him *Al Jauzah*, loosely meaning "the Middle Figure of the Heavens," and *Al Babadur*, "the Strong One."

The Jews called him *Gibbor*, or "the Giant." They also considered him as Nimrod, who was strapped to the great sky dome for rebelling against Jehovah. The Hindus once called him *Praja-pati*, meaning "the Stag." This stag was said to be chasing his own daughter, Aldebaran, but was killed by an arrow shot by Sirius. The arrow can be seen sticking into the stag as Orion's belt stars. These three belt stars have been variously called the Golden Grains, the Golden Walnuts, the Arrow, a Scale Beam, and a Row. Sailors once knew this trio of stars as the Golden Yard Arm. It has also been called the

Magi and the Three Kings.

The brightest star in this constellation is Rigel (magnitude of 0.14), from the Arabic word *rijl*, meaning "leg." So that star forms the left leg, or foot, of the Giant. Rigel is the seventh brightest star in the sky and is a double star, which you can split with a small telescope. Both components are bluish-white stars. There are so many interesting objects to be explored in Orion that you can spend many nights studying the constellation without becoming bored. Don't overlook the bright yellow star Bellatrix (mag. 1.64), which forms the Giant's left shoulder. Above and between Bellatrix and Betelgeuse is a small triangle of stars called Meissa, meaning "the Head of the Giant." In ancient China these stars were called *Si ma Ts'ien*, meaning "the Head of the Tiger," when Orion formed part of a larger constellation recognized by the ancient Chinese as the White Tiger.

The second brightest star in Orion is Betelgeuse (mag. 0.41), which comes from the Arabic *Ibt al Jauzah*, meaning "the Armpit of the Central One."

This star marks the giant's right shoulder and is the upper left member of a four-star quadrangle forming Orion's body. Betelgeuse is a giant red star so large that if it replaced the Sun it would fill our Solar System to out beyond the orbit of Mars, gobbling up Earth, Venus, and Mercury. Betelgeuse is a pulsating variable star.

Opposite Rigel is the star Saiph. The top star of the trio of bright stars forming Orion's belt is called Mintaka. It is a double star, one component being brilliant white and the other being pale violet. The middle belt star is a bright white one called Alnilam (mag. 1.7), from the Arabic *Al Nitham*, meaning "the String of Pearls." The lower belt star is Alnitak, from the Arabic *Al Nitak*, meaning "the Girdle." It is a triple star the components of which are topaz yellow, light purple, and gray.

The misty veil of stars extending downward from Orion's belt forms his sword. You will see what appears to be three stars. But if you look carefully—especially with binoculars—you will see that the middle "star" actually is a foggy patch, the Great

Nebula designated in star catalogs as M 42. It is the most splendid bright nebula visible to us. And it is one of the very few that we can see with the naked eye. Just a bit below and to the right of the lowest star in Orion's belt is another nebula, a dark nebula called the Horsehead Nebula, designated in star catalogs as IC 434.

Don't stop your exploration of Orion here. See what other objects of interest you can discover for yourself.

Orion is best observed from December through March.

PERSEUS ☆☆☆☆☆☆☆☆☆☆☆☆☆☆☆☆☆☆☆☆☆☆☆☆☆☆☆☆☆☆☆☆☆☆☆

When we told the story of Andromeda and her family, we met Perseus (page 39), the young warrior who rescued Andromeda from the sea-monster. Cetus had been sent by Poseidon to devour the girl as she was chained to the rocky coast of her homeland.

It is during this season of the year when Perseus reveals himself to our view high overhead. He

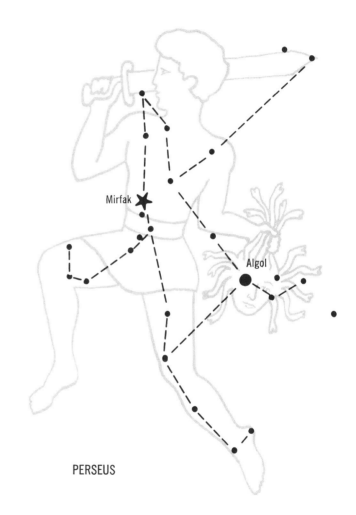

Mirfak

Algol

PERSEUS

usually is pictured with a raised sword in his right hand and the terrible Medusa's head held in his left hand.

Christians have seen David holding the head of Goliath in this group of stars, and others have seen the Apostle Paul with his sword and book. The brightest star in Perseus is Mirfak (magnitude of 1.8), from the Arabic and meaning the Elbow. It is a very bright lilac-colored star. The second brightest star in the constellation is Algol (mag. 2.1), the gleaming eye of the Medusa's head.

TAURUS (the Bull) ☆☆☆☆☆☆☆☆☆☆☆☆☆☆☆☆☆☆☆☆☆☆

The bull long was a symbol of strength and goodness and has played a chief role in the mythologies of cultures from one end of Europe to the other and throughout the Near East. The Bull-god Apis was for thousands of years worshiped in Egypt. To qualify for the honor of being an Apis-bull, a real bull must have certain markings and then be tended by the high priests. For as long as it lived, an Apis-bull supposedly embodied the soul of the Bull-god. When the Apis-bull died, another, with similar markings, had to be found to house the soul of the Bull-god.

Years ago in Memphis, Egypt, archaeologists unearthed the ancient tomb of the Apis-bulls and could hardly believe what they found. Leading to the tomb itself was a broad paved avenue lined by lions carved out of stone. To enter the tomb, one walked through a long and high arched corridor cut into solid rock. It extended for 2,000 feet and was six meters (twenty feet) wide and six meters high. Many recesses along each side of the corridor had been carved into the rock and each held the ornately entombed remains of Apis-bulls as each one died.

Spring was the time when festivals honoring the Apis-bulls were held. It was also a time when the River Nile gently overflowed its banks and brought life-giving moisture to the land, a time for planting to begin. At the time we are now talking about, roughly around 4000 B.C., the Sun's position along the Zodiac on the first day of spring, or Vernal

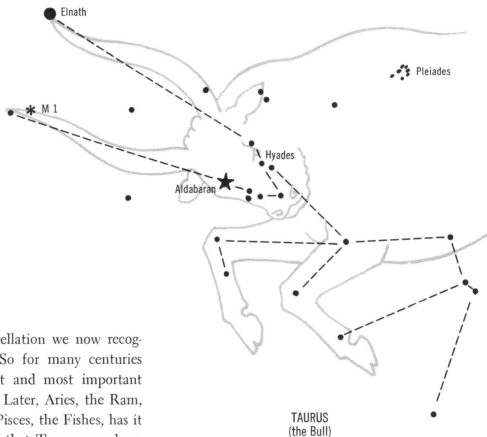

Elnath

Pleiades

M 1

Hyades

Aldabaran

TAURUS
(the Bull)

Equinox, was in that constellation we now recognize as Taurus, the Bull. So for many centuries Taurus was to be the first and most important constellation of the Zodiac. Later, Aries, the Ram, was to have that honor, as Pisces, the Fishes, has it today. Some have suggested that Taurus may have been the first Zodiac constellation invented. But as you will find later, Gemini might have had that honor.

Again, evidence of bull-worship is found in many different cultures over a long period of time and there can be no doubt that it was closely associated with that group of stars through which the Sun passed during Spring Equinox.

So it is not surprising to find that bulls play important roles in early Greek mythology. The Greeks took over the bull as a symbol of power from the Egyptians, as the Egyptians had taken it from the Babylonians, and the Babylonians from the Sumerians.

There are at least two Greek myths in which a bull plays an important role. In one, Zeus falls in love with Europa, the daughter of the king of Tyre. But Europa was constantly guarded by her father's servants. One day Zeus changed himself into a beautiful white bull with golden horns. He then mixed with the royal herds that were grazing in a large field by the sea. Europa, who had been walking along the beach, noticed this beautiful animal and

could not resist going up to it and feeding it. So friendly and gentle was this splendid bull that she climbed onto its back and grasped its golden horns.

Gradually the white bull wandered closer to the sea and when near the beach ran into the water and began swimming toward the island of Crete. By this time it was too late for Europa to climb off.

When the two arrived in Crete, Zeus changed himself back into his own form. Realizing that he could not marry Europa himself, Zeus gave her in marriage to Asterius, king of Crete.

In another Greek myth Zeus falls in love with Io, a priestess of his wife, Hera. For many nights Zeus whispers to Io in her dreams. He tells her to go to the fields beside the river Lerna. Io tells her father, Inachus, about these dreams and asks him what they mean. Inachus consults an oracle who tells him that he must send his daughter away or the great god Zeus will destroy them by hurling down thunderbolts. Amid tears from both Io and her father, she is sent away to wander the land. On seeing the girl now alone, Zeus overtakes and approaches her. But on realizing that his jealous wife Hera is looking on, Zeus quickly changes Io into the form of a white cow.

Now Hera knew that Zeus had a weakness for beautiful women and would run off with one whenever he could. And she knew that he would change Io back into a woman again as soon as he thought he could do so safely. So Hera demanded that Zeus give her, Hera, the beautiful white cow, since it was *only* a cow. What else could Zeus do?

Zeus next sent Hermes to try to steal the white cow but it was constantly guarded by Argus Panoptes, a many-eyed monster who was said never to sleep. But Hermes managed to lull the monster to sleep by telling him stories and playing tunes on his pipe. He then cut off Argus's head and led the white cow away. Now Hera was aware of the plot and next sent down a fierce insect to sting the cow. The cow bolted and escaped from Hermes. She ran and did not stop until she was far away. Then she wandered aimlessly. Now some say that Zeus eventually found Io and transformed himself into a bull to be with her for a while. Others say that he changed her back into a woman and that the two lived together happily awhile, at least until the wrath of Hera brought him home again. At any rate, for the good fortune the form of a bull had brought him, Zeus raised the animal to a place of importance among the stars as Taurus.

The best time to observe Taurus is from October through March.

THE PLEIADES ☆☆☆☆☆☆☆☆☆☆☆☆☆☆☆☆☆☆☆☆☆☆☆☆

The Pleiades, that tiny cluster of stars forming Taurus's left shoulder, is one of the most striking sky objects we can see. It also has played a major role in astronomy over the past several thousands of years. And it most likely was important to people living long before writing was invented.

People the world over long have associated this bright little group of stars with death. It is not hard to understand why. When the Pleiades climbed ever higher in the sky night after night and then

The Pleiades (M 45, or NGC 1432) are a beautiful open star cluster in Taurus, as seen through the 100-inch telescope. See constellation diagram and winter star chart for location. HALE OBSERVATORIES.

The "Crab" Nebula (M 1, or NGC 1952) in Taurus as seen through the 48-inch Schmidt telescope. This nebula marks the remains of a supernova star that was seen to explode in the year 1054. HALE OBSERVATORIES.

reached their highest point on the sky dome, they marked the time when the days were growing shorter. This was the time when the Sun was low in the sky and becoming "weaker," and when the cold dry season gripped the land. Crops ceased to grow, and in the high latitudes a blanket of snow snuffed out life for a while. Indeed, it was a time of death. It was also the time when the souls of the dead left Earth for the Underworld. They fled at midnight when the Pleiades hung menacingly overhead. It was also a time to appease the dark gods of the night, a time when witches and the monster clan of Ti'amat were at their strongest, a time to perform human sacrifices to assure the return of light and the renewal of growth and warmth. Our Halloween and Feast of All Souls are but two of the many observations of this dreaded time made by people the world over. While today children in many places dance around a bonfire to celebrate this day, centuries ago human sacrifices were offered up to the flames of those bonfires.

The Aztecs, for example, offered human sacrifices on this day to prevent the end of the world from occurring, as they said that it had once long, long ago. The sacrificial victim was strapped down to the altar and a fire lighted over his heart. Firewood was added stick-by-stick until the flames from his body and the wood reached their greatest height at the moment the Pleiades were seen to cross the exact overhead position. If the timing was right, and if the sacrificial victim proved to be worthy of the sacrifice, then all went well. Since the end of the world did not come about again, this was proof that the sacrifices worked!

The Egyptians, the ancient Britains, the Mexicans, Chinese, Japanese, and others all observed this dreaded time when the Pleiades reached their highest overhead position, or *culminated*, as astronomers say. Nearly all of these festivals marking the culmination of the Pleiades took place in November, the month when we still see the Pleiades best.

It is not surprising to find that people living in the Southern Hemisphere celebrated the culmination of the Pleiades for just the opposite reason. For "down under" the Pleiades marked the coming of summer and end of winter. So for these people the Pleiades represented light, warmth, and a rebirth of life.

There is still another way of observing the Pleiades—during that time of the year when they first appear over the horizon just before the Sun rises. This is called their *heliacal* rising (from the word Helios, the Greek Sun-god). When observed at this time, the Pleiades signal the time for agricultural activities to begin and they mark the seasonal rebirth. Around 2700 B.C. the heliacal rising of the Pleiades came right in step with Spring Equinox when it occurred in Taurus. So the Pleiades have two aspects, a good aspect when observed at their heliacal rising, and a bad aspect when observed as they reach culmination.

There are numerous North American and South American myths accounting for the Pleiades. For example, the Blackfoot Indians tell of six brothers whose family was very poor and could not provide the boys with the kind of buffalo robes worn by other boys in the tribe. Saddened, and out of shame, the six boys went up to the sky where they became the "Bunched Stars," or Pleiades.

A Polynesian myth accounting for the Pleiades says that long ago the six stars in that group were one star, a star so beautiful that it loudly boasted that it was the most beautiful star in the heavens, more beautiful even than the nearby Sirius and Aldebaran. Now the other stars eventually grew tired of hearing the loud boasting of the ill-mannered star and appealed to the great god Tane. After considering the matter for a long time, Tane decided to act. So he picked up Aldebaran and hurled that star with all his might at the large, braggart star. Aldebaran was a tough star and was delighted to have been chosen as the missile to punish the large star. On colliding with the large star, Aldebaran was not harmed, but the large star was shattered into six smaller stars. The other stars were pleased and thanked Tane. It is said to this day, however, that if you listen carefully on a clear night, you can hear the six little stars whispering among themselves that now they are even lovelier than before since they are now six instead of one. In Polynesia, the Pleiades cluster is known as *Matariki*, meaning "Little Eyes."

It is interesting that this myth, along with the Blackfoot myth, mentions only six stars forming this cluster. The ancient Greeks, Egyptians, and Hindus mentioned seven stars. It is thought that the seven chambers of the Great Pyramid represented the seven stars of the Pleiades. And this cluster represents the seven sisters of the Hindus who married the seven sages of Ursa Major. At that time the seventh star, which we see dimly today, may have been brighter than it is now.

In Greek mythology the Pleiades were seven daughters of the Creator-god Atlas and his wife Pleione. It is said that Zeus raised them to the heavens as stars to protect them from Orion, who for seven long years pursued the maidens, and Pleione, to claim them for himself. Another version of the myth says that Zeus elevated them to stardom when they died of grief over the death of the Hyades, their half-sisters.

THE HYADES ☆☆☆☆☆☆☆☆☆☆☆☆☆☆☆☆☆☆☆☆☆☆☆☆☆☆☆☆

As early as 100 B.C. Chinese astronomers had recognized this cluster of five stars forming the head of Taurus. Records show that the ancient Chinese were performing sacrifices in honor of these stars, which represented their god Yu Shih, God of Rain.

Long, long ago, the Chinese myth tells us, the goddess Nu Kua created the world out of chaos. Jealous of her powers, the forces of evil rose up against her and set about destroying the world. Their leader was the giant god Kung Kung, who commanded the realm of oceans and all watery things. Kung Kung caused a great flood during which the sea rose up into great whirlpools and began to destroy the world.

Nu Kua was joined in her battle against Kung Kung by the Fire-god, who helped her tame the seas and restore the world. Kung Kung was thoroughly defeated and sent off into exile in the dark regions far beyond the heavens. On leaving, the evil god passed on his powers over the oceans and all watery things to his son, Yu Shih, who made his home in the Hyades. Unlike his evil father, Yu Shih became man's friend and brought him water when he most needed it.

According to Greek myth, the Hyades were the half-sisters of the Pleiades. Now the Hyades had a brother named Hyas, of whom they were very fond. One day while out hunting, Hyas was killed by a lion. When word of his death reached his sisters, they all died of grief. Feeling sorry for them, Zeus placed them in the heavens as that cluster we now call the Hyades.

We could go on and spin still other myths about the constellation Taurus since so many peoples throughout history have recognized him. He was known as *Al Thaur* by the Arabs, *Il Toro* by the Italians, *Le Taureau* by the French, *Taura* by the Persians, and *Shor* by the Jews. In China the constellation, along with Orion, formed the White Tiger. The Roman poets spoke of Taurus, otherwise a rather dull constellation, as being "rich in maidens."

When you look for Taurus in the sky, don't expect to find the entire bull. You are supposed to see only his front half. The explanation is that his hind quarters are underwater since he is quite busy carrying Europa across the sea to Crete. And don't really expect to see the shape of the front quarters of a bull, except in your imagination.

What you *will* see without too much trouble is a V-shape cluster of five bright stars, the Hyades. The brightest one of these is Aldebaran (magnitude of 0.9), which forms Taurus's glaring red right eye. The V-shape forms his face. The Pleiades cluster forms the bull's left shoulder. As the stars parade across the heavens Taurus is seen to move backward, as if fleeing from the upraised club of neighboring Orion.

The brightest star in Taurus is the bright red Aldebaran, from the Arabic *Al Dabaran*, meaning "the Follower" (it is following the Pleiades). Called the "Seven Sisters," the Pleiades make a very pretty cluster. You probably won't have trouble counting four or five stars in this group. If you can see six you don't have to worry about your eyesight. Some people can make out a very dim seventh star, the so-called Lost Pleiade of legend. Binoculars will reveal many more stars in this fine cluster.

The second brightest star in this constellation is Elnath (mag. 1.7), from the Arabic *Al Natih,* meaning "the Butting One," because this star forms the tip of the bull's left horn.

It is the Hyades that supposedly give the bull its distinctive face-shape. Several cultures far removed from each other have seen the face of a bull in this star cluster. The ancient Chinese called it the Golden Ox. And in the faraway valley of the Amazon the South American Indians called it the Jawbone of an Ox. There are five fairly easily visible stars here. But, as with the Pleiades, binoculars will reveal more.

Near the bull's right horn is another interesting sky object, the Crab Nebula, or M 1. It is the remains of a giant star which Chinese astronomers in the year 1054 saw explode as a supernova star. Today its remains of gas and dust continue to spread out at the rate of about 800 miles a second. It is now more than 4.2 light-years in diameter.

AURIGA (the Charioteer) ☆☆☆☆☆☆☆☆☆☆☆☆☆☆☆☆☆☆☆

The star Elnath, forming the northern horn of Taurus, also forms the left foot of Auriga, the Charioteer, while the very bright star, Capella, forms the Charioteer's right shoulder. Auriga is pretty much of a mystery constellation for several reasons. First of all, it is one of the oldest constellations, going back at least to Babylonian times. And it has always been associated with a charioteer, although there is nothing whatever in the five or so stars that make it up to remind us of a chariot, or its driver.

Even so, down through the years the Babylonians, Greeks, Arabs, and even the faraway Chinese have associated this constellation with a chariot. Usually what is shown is a man holding reins and a whip, as if ready to harness the missing horses and climb into the nonexistent chariot. Then if you look closely you will see a goat supported on the charioteer's shoulder. And held in his right hand behind his back are two kids.

Capella, Auriga's brightest star, along with the Pleiades and Hyades, has long been associated with light spring rains. Perhaps this is one reason why it has for so long been known as the "Shepherd's Star," since spring rains mean lush pasturelands for the shepherds' flocks.

According to one Greek myth, Hera, Goddess of Heaven, had a child who was born lame. Disgusted, she threw him down out of Heaven to Earth, where he became the famous lame smith, Hephaestus, who fashioned beautiful ornaments and armor for the gods. He is also the smith who came to Orion's rescue after Orion had been blinded (see page 122). It is said that because he was lame he invented the chariot so that he might get around better.

Auriga's brightest star gets its name from the Romans and means "Little She-goat." Capella (magnitude 0.05) marks the goat resting on Auriga's

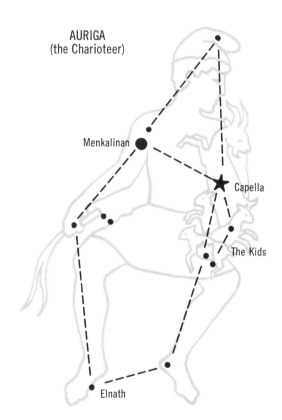

AURIGA
(the Charioteer)

Menkalinan

Capella

The Kids

Elnath

shoulder. The Arabs knew the star as *Al Rakib*, or "the Driver." This particular Driver was not driving Greek sheep but Arabian camels represented by the Pleiades. The ancient Chinese saw Capella as one of the stars in a constellation they called *Woo Chay*, or "the Five Chariots" [of the Five Emperors].

The second brightest star in this constellation is the bright yellow star Menkalinan (mag. 1.9) marking the left shoulder of Auriga. Try scanning the inside rectangle formed by Auriga's shoulder-stars and foot-stars with binoculars. You are bound to find several interesting star clusters and a number of double stars. Also try to locate the small triangle of stars known as the Kids.

GEMINI (the Twins) ☆☆☆☆☆☆☆☆☆☆☆☆☆☆☆☆☆☆☆☆☆☆☆☆☆

Just to the left of Auriga is the famous Zodiac constellation of the Twins, whose heads are the two very bright stars Pollux and Castor. They form the brightest close pair of stars seen from the Northern Hemisphere. It's pretty hard to miss this constellation once you have located Orion.

As with so many others of the constellations, there are differing versions of how Castor and Pollux gained stardom. There are so many versions, in fact, that you can play "Dial-a-Myth" with them. According to one Greek myth, the following events came to pass.

The Twins were sons of Zeus and the mortal Leda. Pollux had an immortal soul, so on his death he was assured of a place in Heaven with the gods. However, Castor had a mortal soul and so was destined for Hades along with the rest of mankind. Nevertheless, in all other respects,

> So like they were, no mortal
> Might one from the other know.

Castor became famous as a rider of horses, while his brother Pollux became equally skilled at boxing and fighting battles. Eventually they decided to take wives and selected the two beautiful daughters of the king of Sparta. Now it happened that the two women were already married to Lynceus and Idas, cousins of the Twins. But this seems to have made

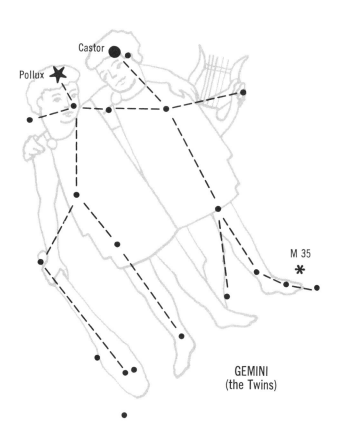

Castor

Pollux

M 35

*

GEMINI
(the Twins)

little difference to the Twins. They simply carried the girls off and settled down with them. The two cousins seem not to have been bothered by the theft of their wives and left the Twins alone. A few years later, the cousins, in the friendly company of the Twins, made a joint raid on some cattle. It is said that trouble between the two pairs of thieves began when they tried to divide the cattle among themselves.

Idas had the solution. He hacked one of the cows into four equal pieces and said that whichever two individuals completely finished eating their quarters first would divide the spoils. This took the Twins off guard and they watched helplessly as their two cousins wolfed down their quarters of the cow. Idas and Lynceus then drove off the entire herd.

Tricked, Castor and Pollux vowed to get even with their cousins. Within a few days they set out after Lynceus and Idas to recover their share of the cattle. During the fight that followed, Idas killed Castor with a spear. Infuriated over the loss of his twin brother, Pollux chased his cousins and killed

Lynceus with a single blow. Just as Idas was about to hurl a tombstone at Pollux, Zeus came to Pollux's aid and hurled a thunderbolt at Idas, killing him on the spot.

Realizing that his brother's soul would go to Hades, Pollux prayed to his father and asked that he, too, be killed and his soul sent to Hades so that he would not be parted from his brother. Even the great Zeus was not able to grant such a wish, but he told Pollux that there was a way the boys could be together. Half the time they would spend together in Hades and the other half on Olympus with the gods. In addition, both would be given a place in the sky as the constellation Gemini.

To this day we see the Twins there, guardians of sailors threatened by storms at sea. It is said that even in our times the Twins sometimes appear to us as those mysterious balls of fire, called Saint Elmo's Fire, that are seen in the rigging of ships during electrical storms. If only one ball is seen, it is a bad omen. If two balls are seen it is a sign that the Twins are looking after the ship.

Last night I saw Saint Elmo's stars,
  With their glittering lanterns all at play
On the tops of the masts and the tips of the spars,
  And I knew we should have foul weather to-day.

The Blackfoot Indians also have a legend accounting for Pollux and Castor. In brief, it tells of a wandering medicine man who visits a woman and her two infants one day while her husband is off hunting. The medicine man kills the woman and, before leaving, places one of the infants by the ashes of the fire in the tipi and sticks the other behind a buffalo skin. He then gives the infants the names Ashes-Chief and Stuck-Behind.

The boys' father was not much interested in raising the infants and left them on their own. It turned out that one was raised by a rock and the other by a beaver. Both were given magical powers and were involved in several interesting adventures as they grew up. Eventually, when they died they rose into the sky as the Twins.

In ancient China the Twins were known as Yin

and Yang. These are two mystical elements of the Universe, elements of opposites that have always played an important part in religions of the world—day and night, the powers of darkness and light, good and evil, and all sorts of other opposites. Yin is said to be female and represents darkness and cold, the Moon and winter. Yang is said to be male and represents light, the Sun, life, summer, and so on. Separated, the two principles are said to be meaningless; but together they give meaning to the Universe.

In addition to myths surrounding the Twins are stone carvings left to us by the ancient Babylonians. They show an upturned crescent Moon with its tips pointing one to Castor and the other to Pollux. Why should this be especially interesting? As mentioned earlier, when the Sun appears in Pisces, it signals the beginning of spring, Vernal Equinox, after which the days begin to grow longer and are longer than night. Centuries ago, Spring Equinox occurred in the constellation Aries, and before that in Taurus. We now know that in even earlier times

Spring Equinox occurred in Gemini, and at a time when the two "horns" of the Moon pointed toward the Twins. Although the Babylonian stones are only 3,500 years old, the astronomical picture they show us is much older and must have been handed down to the Babylonians by much earlier people who were expert stargazers. Since Spring Equinox once occurred in Gemini, it is highly likely that people who lived before writing was invented recognized this important celestial event. It also is highly likely that they associated a constellation with it.

At one time or another, the Egyptians have pictured Gemini as two closely related gods, Horus the Elder, and Horus the Younger, and as the Two Sprouting Plants. Arabian astronomers have known Gemini as *Al Tau'aman*, "the Twins," and the Persians have called them *Du Paikar*, "the Two Figures." They also have been seen as the Pair of Kids, presumably following Auriga with his goat, and as the Two Gazelles.

The brightest star in Gemini is the orange Pollux

(magnitude of 1.2), although it may have gained the number-one position only in the past few hundred years. Castor (mag. 2.5) is the next brightest, for now at least, and is a bright white double star, but you need a telescope to see it as two stars. Once you learn to trace the outline of this constellation, look just above the left foot of Castor and try to find M 35. Binoculars will reveal this naked-eye fuzzy patch as a fine star cluster.

Gemini is best observed from December through May.

CANIS MINOR (the Little Dog) ☆☆☆☆☆☆☆☆☆☆☆☆☆☆
CANIS MAJOR (the Big Dog) ☆☆☆☆☆☆☆☆☆☆☆☆☆☆☆

What makes these two constellations interesting is the fact that they contain two of the brightest stars visible to us, Sirius and Procyon. The many myths associated with Canis Major and Canis Minor have more to tell us about these two brilliant stars than about the constellations of which they are a part.

Both the Big Dog and Little Dog are said to have been the pets of a variety of gods and goddesses. Among the various owners named are Helen, Ulixes, Europa, Icarus, and others. Usually, however, the two dogs are regarded as the faithful hunting hounds of the giant Orion. This is reflected in an Arabic title for the constellation, *Al Kalb al Jabbar*, or "the Dog of the Giant." Sirius (magnitude of —1.5), the brightest star seen in the night sky, forms the nose of Canis Major. A triangle of somewhat less bright stars forms the hind quarters of the dog.

For centuries Sirius has been known as the Dog Star. The Greeks seem not to have seen a constellation here but were concerned only with the star Sirius. Long ago the Australian aborigines knew Sirius as their Eagle, a constellation by itself. Not until some time later did the Romans associate other nearby stars with Sirius and Procyon and picture the two as parts of dog figures. Arabian astronomers went along with this notion and so called the constellations *Al Kalb al Akbar*, or "the Greater Dog," and *Al Kalb al Asghar*, "the Lesser Dog."

It was once believed that the intense heat of summer drove dogs mad. And since Sirius is associated with the hot months of July and August, because it appears closest to the Sun then, it became known as the Dog Star. The Romans used to sacrifice a fawn-colored dog to Sirius once each year. The purpose of the sacrifice was to prevent this "heat star" from scorching their crops and drying up the land. At the time the Romans worshiped this star, Sirius reportedly was red in color, but now it is bluish-white.

Sirius's intense brightness is due to the star being so close to us, less than nine light-years away. This makes it the fifth closest star, not counting the Sun. Because it is the brightest star in the night sky, it is not surprising to find that it was worshiped by many cultures long before it was made part of a constellation. The Egyptian records show that the rising of Sirius at dawn was used by the astronomer-priests at least as early as 3000 B.C. The day on which Sirius was first seen to rise at dawn became New Year's Day for the Egyptians, and they called Sirius "Mistress of the Year." In honor of Sirius, the Egyptians oriented temples so that they faced that point on the horizon where Sirius was first seen to rise at dawn. One such temple was built as early as 2700 B.C.

In Egyptian mythology Sirius was associated with Isis, Goddess of Fertility. When her husband Osiris died, it is said that the tears of Isis caused the Nile to overflow its banks. The ancient Egyptians also believed that the world was created when Sirius first rose with the Sun.

The second brightest star in Canis Major is a white one marking the dog's left paw and is called Murzim (mag. 2.0), from the Arabic *Al Murzim*, or "the Announcer," meaning that the rising of Murzim announces the immediate rising of His Honor, Sirius. With binoculars try to find M 41 in this constellation. It is a lovely star cluster with a red star near its center.

If you look directly ahead of the Big Dog's nose you will find that his attention is focused not on his master Orion, but on Lepus, the Hare. This is a small and dim constellation. Its two brightest stars are Arneb and Nihal, which form one edge of a small dipperlike rectangle. It seems fitting that a hare is found near the giant Hunter and one of his hounds.

Canis Minor is a pretty pale invention of the Romans. Nothing short of the magic of Jupiter can produce a dog here, although you won't have trouble finding the bright star Procyon (magnitude of 0.4). One way to find this yellowish-white star, which happens to be a double star, is to remember that it forms an equal-sided triangle with Sirius and Betelgeuse, in Orion. The second brightest star in this constellation is a white star called Gomeisa (mag. 2.9). It has also been called Al Murzim right along with the Al Murzim of Canis Major, and for the same reason.

Because Sirius and Procyon are seen on opposite sides of the Milky Way, there are a number of myths describing how these two companions became separated by the great Sky River. The Arabs tell of two sisters who tried to follow their brother across the sky. When they came to the great Sky River they plunged in to swim across. The older and stronger sister, Sirius, managed and today can be seen on the southern bank of that great river. But the younger sister was too weak and remained weeping on the northern bank, where we still see her today as Procyon. Perhaps her tears, like those of Isis, contribute to the seasonal flooding of the Nile.

Canis Major and the Hare he is chasing are best seen from January through March. The Little Dog is best seen along with the Twins from December through May.

CANCER (the Crab) ☆☆☆☆☆☆☆☆☆☆☆☆☆☆☆☆☆☆☆☆☆☆☆☆☆

This is the faintest of the twelve Zodiac constellations, and most amateur astronomers choose to pass it by. But for your own satisfaction you should at least know that you can locate it, if you had to in an emergency. It lies midway between Gemini and Canis Minor and a bit to the left and just above the head of Hydra. Now don't expect to find this constellation unless seeing conditions are just about perfect—a clear sky, no Moon, and no city lights.

The Tropic of Cancer was named after this constellation centuries ago when Summer Solstice occurred there. The Tropic of Cancer is the northernmost latitude at which the Sun appears directly overhead, which is 23½° N. Among Cancer's stars is the famous Gate of Men. Each newborn babe supposedly received a mortal soul which descended from Heaven, passing through the Gate of Men on the way. When a person died, the soul supposedly passed through a similar stellar gate

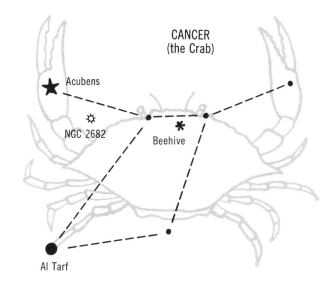

CANCER
(the Crab)

Acubens

NGC 2682

Beehive

Al Tarf

An open star cluster (M 67, or NGC 2682) in Cancer, as seen through the 200-inch telescope. These clusters have up to about 1000 stars. See constellation diagram and winter star chart for location. HALE OBSERVATORIES.

on its way back up to Heaven. That gate was located at the opposite point on the sky, in Capricorn, after which the Tropic of Capricon was named. The Tropic of Capricorn is the southernmost latitude at which the Sun is ever seen directly overhead, which is 23½° S.

The brightest star in Cancer is a fourth magnitude star called Acubens, from the Arabic *Al Zubanah,* meaning "the Claws," and it marks the southern claw of the Crab. It is a double star, one component of which is white and the other red. The second brightest star is *Al Tarf,* also of fourth magnitude, meaning "the End," and it forms the tip of the fifth and lowest left leg of this fierce beast who joined the dreaded Hydra in battle against Hercules (see page 64).

Once you have learned to find the lopsided square forming the body of the Crab, see if you can find the so-called Beehive, a faint patch of light which binoculars will reveal as an open cluster of stars that appears as a swarm of bees. Other designations for the Beehive are M 44 and Praesepe.

Cancer's chief claim to fame is that in the year 1531 Halley's Comet was discovered in this part of the sky. And then, in the summer of 1895, all of the planets, except Neptune, congregated here—an extremely rare event.

Cancer is best observed from January through May.

ERIDANUS (the River) ☆☆☆☆☆☆☆☆☆☆☆☆☆☆☆☆☆☆☆☆☆☆☆

Like a real river, this celestial River of Heaven, or Great River of the Sky, meanders all over. It is not easy to find and you may well give up discouraged. But you should be able to trace at least part of it by finding its point of termination just above the star Rigel in Orion. From here follow it upstream as it meanders westward and then loops around to the south and east and then loops again to the south and west and disappears down over the southern horizon where its source lies.

This Great River of the Sky has been identified with several real Earth rivers throughout history. It might represent the Sumerian Strong River, also

Cursa

ERIDANUS
(the River)

Achernar

known as Ariadan. Or it might be one or more of any other number of important rivers—the Ganges, Po, Euphrates, or Nile.

In Greek mythology the flippant son of the Sun-god Apollo was unable to control the Sun-chariot of his father. When it got out of control and threatened to destroy Earth, Zeus hurled a thunderbolt at the boy and killed him. His burning body fell into the River Eridanus (see page 56).

The brightest star in Eridanus is Achernar (magnitude of 0.5), from the Arabic *Al Ahir al Nahr*, meaning "the End of the River." Unfortunately this star is very low in the sky and is not visible from any farther north than a latitude of about 30° N, which is on a line with New Orleans.

The second brightest star in this wet constellation is the topaz-yellow star Cursa (mag. 2.8), which marks the river's end point.

The Spring Sky

As spring rolls around, our old friends of winter and earlier will slip away, or partly so. You will still see part of the Northern Crown, Libra, and the Great Bear, for example. But the central part of the sky will be occupied by a group of newcomers, some of them splendid constellations. But perhaps the greatest joy in exploring the spring sky is because its numerous figures are heralds of warm weather, gentle rains, and a rebirth of the world.

One of the major constellations you will find is Leo, the Lion, which is easy to pick out because of his distinctive sickle, which forms his head, and the equally distinctive triangle forming his hindquarters and tail. Two beautiful bright stars, Regulus and Denebola, help make Leo a brilliant constellation.

In the opposite part of the sky from Leo is Boötes, the Herdsman, with his brilliant golden-orange star Arcturus. Southwest of Boötes is Virgo, the Virgin, also sporting a brilliant star, Spica. And beneath them all is the many-headed monster which Hercules had to do battle with—Hydra, the longest

The "Whirlpool" Galaxy (M 51, or NGC 5194), a spiral galaxy found near Boötes, as seen through the 200-inch telescope. Its accompanying satellite galaxy is NGC 5195. See spring star chart for location. HALE OBSERVATORIES.

A spherical galaxy (M 87, or NGC 4486) in Virgo, as seen through the 200-inch telescope. See constellation diagram and spring star chart for location. HALE OBSERVATORIES.

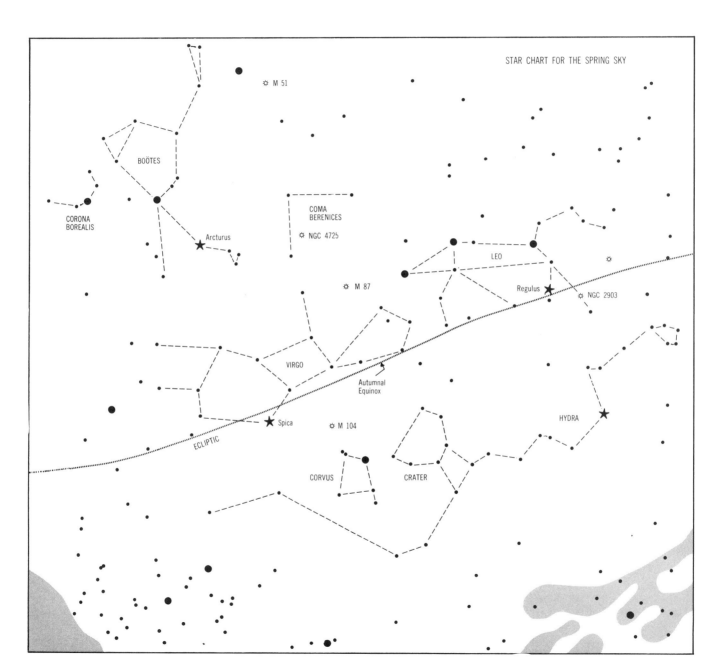

STAR CHART FOR THE SPRING SKY

☆ M 51

BOÖTES

CORONA
BOREALIS

Arcturus

COMA
BERENICES

☆ NGC 4725

☆ M 87

LEO

Regulus ☆ NGC 2903

VIRGO

Autumnal
Equinox

HYDRA

Spica

☆ M 104

ECLIPTIC

CORVUS

CRATER

constellation in the heavens. If you have a telescope you should be able to make out three impressive spring sky objects, M 51, M 87, and M 104, three spectacular galaxies.

BOÖTES *(the Herdsman)* ☆☆☆☆☆☆☆☆☆☆☆☆☆☆☆☆☆☆☆☆☆

In late spring, right after sunset, look high up in the sky and you will see a very bright star. It will be Arcturus and is the key star to help you find the Herdsman. Picture him as an upside-down necktie with Arcturus at the neck-end of the tie. At the tip-end is a star marking the Herdsman's forehead. As

the tie broadens, its two broadest points have stars marking the Herdsman's shoulders. Keeping that general outline in mind should enable you to pick out Boötes quickly and easily.

The name "Boötes" is at least 3,000 years old, but in those ancient times the name most likely applied to the star Arcturus rather than to the entire group of stars we include today.

According to Greek myth, there were two Athenians, Icarius and his daughter Erigone, who welcomed a visit by Dionysos, the God of Wine. Grateful for being treated so well by the Athenians, Dionysos taught Icarius the art of growing grapes for wine making.

After successfully making wine, Icarius set out with his daughter and dog Maera to teach others over the countryside how to grow wine grapes. He took with him several containers of wine so that others might taste its excellence. Now the three came upon a group of shepherds and told them about making wine. Icarius also left them a container of wine which the shepherds drank. Now

The spring star chart shows only those constellation figures mentioned in the text, although numerous additional stars are shown. All star-shaped stars represent stars of magnitude 1.5 and brighter. The large-dot stars represent stars of magnitude 2 to 2.5. The small-dot stars represent stars with magnitudes less than 2.5. Note the long broken line representing the ecliptic. Expect to find the planets along and near this ecliptic-line. The light shaded area represents the Milky Way.

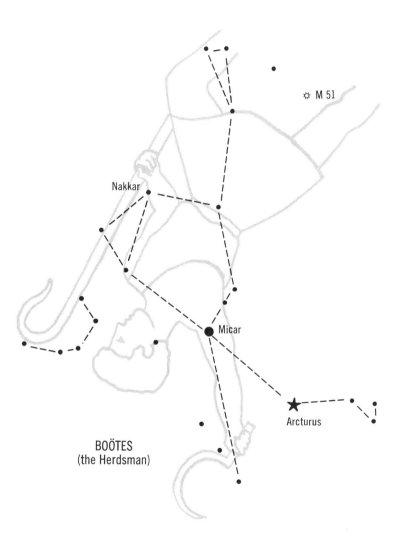

☼ M 51

Nakkar

Micar

★
Arcturus

BOÖTES
(the Herdsman)

they had not diluted the strong wine with water as Icarius had instructed. When they awoke the next morning all of them were ill and thought that Icarius had tried to poison them. The shepherds soon overtook Icarius and pounced on him. With clubs and their fists they beat him to death and then buried him under a tree.

Now Erigone had not been present to witness this terrible act and could not imagine where her father had gone. Maera, Icarius's dog, on being told to go find his master, located the buried body of Icarius. So grief-stricken was Erigone that she hanged herself from the tree marking her father's grave. The dog also is said to have been so grief-stricken that he committed suicide by jumping down a nearby well.

Now when word of the death of Icarius, his daughter, and dog reached Dionysos, the god was furious and promised to avenge his friends. Immediately he cast a spell over all the maidens of Athens, a spell that began to cause the girls to hang themselves from trees. Alarmed by these mass suicides and unable to stop them, a group of the Athenians consulted an oracle. The oracle told them that the girls were committing suicide because the murderers of Icarius had not yet been punished.

No time was lost in finding the guilty shepherds and punishing them. Thereafter the Athenians regularly observed Icarius's death each year during grape harvest, as they do to this day. At each one of these "Swinging Festivals," as they came to be called, young girls swing from trees, either on board-seat swings or by ropes, in memory of the death of Erigone. Dionysos also gave the three honored places among the stars. Icarius became Boötes, the Herdsman. Erigone became the constellation Virgo, the Virgin. And the dog Maera became the Dog Star, Sirius (see also Canis Major, page 141).

The Egyptians believed that those north circumpolar stars that never set over the horizon, but instead remained visible all year as they circled the North Celestial Pole, were evil. And one of the most evil of these northern constellations was the Great Bear. Boötes, they believed, was placed in the sky to guard the Great Bear and see that she did no harm. The Egyptians pictured Boötes as a constellation they called the Hippopotamus. The ancient Greeks at one time also knew Boötes as the Bear Watcher, or Bear Guard. Both the Hindus and ancient Chinese regarded Arcturus as a pearl-star. In Chinese myth, a huge dragon was eternally chasing and trying to capture this star.

Just off to the right of Boötes is M 51, the Whirlpool Galaxy, especially interesting because a satellite galaxy seems to be spinning off from an arm of the main galaxy.

The golden-orange Arcturus (magnitude of —0.06), the brightest star in Boötes, was dreaded by many who thought it brought drought, disease, and other ills associated with the hottest time of the year. But to the astrologers, Arcturus brought riches and honor to those born under its influence. The star's name comes from the Greek words *arktos* and *ouros*, meaning "Bear Watcher" and dating from the time this star by itself was regarded as the constellation.

Arcturus is a famous star, along with Sirius and Betelgeuse, for a reason other than its brightness. Until only a little more than 150 years ago astronomers generally had two classes of stars—the "fixed" stars and the "wanderers." The wanderers, of course, were the planets, which could be seen to move among the so-called fixed stars. The astronomer Edmond Halley, around the year 1718, was able to say that the stars were not fixed, but moved. He did not mean their apparent motion of parading across the sky as a group, a motion due to Earth's turning on its axis. Instead, he meant their motion in relation to each other.

Halley made this discovery by studying star charts drawn up by the Greeks about 1,500 years earlier. These charts showed accurately the positions of Arcturus, Sirius, Betelgeuse, and certain other especially bright stars. Halley next compared those positions with positions on charts he and other astronomers of his time had drawn up. There could be no doubt. Those stars had moved noticeably over that period of time. This meant, of course, that the constellations were slowly changing, as they always have been.

Competing for second brightest status in Boötes is the star Nakkar (mag. 3.5), from the Arabic *Al Nakkar*, "the Digger." The star forms the Herdsman's head, or tip of the necktie. Like Arcturus, it is golden-orange in color, although not as bright as Arcturus.

The best time to observe Boötes is from April through August.

VIRGO (the Virgin) ☆☆☆☆☆☆☆☆☆☆☆☆☆☆☆☆☆☆☆☆☆☆☆

We could easily fill a book about the tales spun about the Zodiac constellation Virgo. She has been identified with numerous goddesses and mortals. She has been Persephone, daughter of the Earth-goddess Demeter; Erigone, daughter of Icarius; Justa, the Roman Goddess of Justice; Astraea, the starry daughter of Themis, mother of the seasons; Isis, the Egyptian Goddess of Fertility; the Virgin Mary; and Eostre, the Saxon Goddess of Spring.

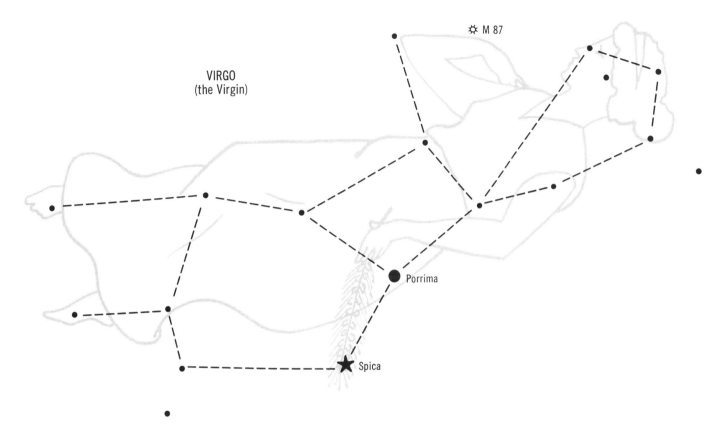

VIRGO
(the Virgin)

☼ M 87

Porrima

Spica

We continue to celebrate the festival of Eostre to this day as Easter, although we observe it for different reasons now. Nevertheless, our observance has its roots in the pre-Christian era when gods and goddesses ruled supreme.

We can trace Virgo as an Earth-goddess associated with the arrival of spring back at least to Sumerian times. Most likely she had her origin several thousands of years earlier still. It now seems likely that people had become farmers at least 10,000 years, and possibly 15,000 years ago. It happens that nearly 15,000 years ago the Sun was in the constellation of Virgo at the Spring Equinox. For some, this would be a time to plant, and for others it would be a time to harvest, as it was for the ancient Egyptians. In either event it would be a time of celebration, a time to honor the all-powerful Earth-goddess.

The earliest such Earth-goddess we have records of is the one probably coming from the Sumerians and called Ishtar by the later Babylonians. We are told that Ishtar's husband, Tammuz died and was destined to spend eternity in the dark underworld. Now Ishtar loved her husband very much and realized that the only way she could get him back was to make the long journey through the Seven Gates to the Underworld, which she did. As soon as she passed through the first gate her absence from Earth caused winter to grip the land and spread its cloak of death.

When Ishtar managed to find the Queen of the Underworld, Eresh-ki-gal, she explained that she wished her husband restored to life. Eresh-ki-gal said that would be quite impossible, that no such request had ever been granted. Now Ishtar was not one to give up easily and remained there pleading her case. Days, weeks, and then months passed. Winter did not leave the Earth above. Crops did not grow, animals did not bear young, and the cloak of death remained over the land.

Alarmed over this situation, the other gods realized that they must do something or the world would come to an end. So they sent a messenger to the first gate where the gatekeeper was told to inform Eresh-ki-gal that it was the will of all the gods that Ishtar return to Earth's surface. Each gatekeeper in turn passed along the message until it was delivered to the great queen herself. Knowing full well that the gods of Heaven were more powerful than she was, she granted Ishtar her wish. As Ishtar and Tammuz made their way up toward Earth's surface, winter's cloak of death slowly melted away.

By the time they reached the first gate the Sun had risen high overhead and the fields had turned green. And by the time they emerged into the bright sunshine and warmth the fields were rich with newly sprouted grains. Spring had come.

Now it is said that so great was the favor done for Ishtar by the Queen of the Underworld that once each year Ishtar must leave Earth for a while to pay her respects to Eresh-ki-gal. When she is gone the cloak of death once again covers the land, but each time she returns life springs anew.

This basic myth has been embroidered and retold by many different peoples who have adopted it as their own, weaving it into their own folklore. The Earth-goddess Virgo was Isis, the Goddess of Fertility, for the ancient Egyptians. Like Ishtar, Isis lost her husband, Osiris, and had to abandon her duties to find him. On one of her travels across the heavens, Isis, who was carrying a sheaf of wheat, accidentally shook the sheaf and scattered the wheat grains. The grains spread around the heavens and we see them today as the Milky Way. That is why

Virgo usually is shown carrying two sheaves of wheat, one of which is marked by the bright star Spica, whose name comes from the Latin and means ear of wheat, or corn.

The Egyptian goddess Isis and the Greek goddess Demeter have much in common. Some have suggested that possibly the ancient Greeks took over Isis as their own Earth-goddess and dressed her in the clothes of Demeter. Demeter, it turns out, spent much time rejoining her lost daughter Persephone, in the same way as Isis and Ishtar did in rejoining their husbands.

We are told that one day when Hades was taking a brief holiday from his duties as God of the Underworld, he saw Persephone and instantly fell in love with her. He promised himself that he would one day marry her and take her down to the Underworld to be his queen. Now Zeus, Persephone's father, thought that Hades would make a good husband for Persephone, but warned that Demeter would never stand for it, since she had to be close to her daughter.

Hades was not discouraged. One day when he knew Persephone was gathering flowers in the field he sped out of the Underworld in his black chariot drawn by four great black horses in golden harness and reins. He sped past Persephone, catching and carrying the girl off with him back to the Underworld.

When her daughter failed to return home, Demeter began to worry, and when Persephone did not return the following day, Demeter set out to find her. For nine days and nights she wandered over the land without food or sleep. Eventually she learned the fate of Persephone. When Zeus pleaded with Demeter to return to Olympus and accept Persephone's marriage to Hades, she refused and continued to roam the land in an attempt to regain Persephone. Her grief became so great that eventually she brought famine all over the land for a full year. People everywhere were starving and could not understand how their Earth-goddess could be so cruel. Alarmed over Demeter's deed, Zeus persuaded all the other gods to go down to Demeter and plead with her to forget her anger and once again take up her position on Olympus so that the crops would grow again. But she refused.

Zeus next sent Hermes, Messenger of the Gods, to visit Hades and tell him that Persephone must return with him. Hades, knowing that the gods of Heaven were stronger than he, agreed to let Persephone go. There was a happy reunion, but Persephone told her mother that she loved her husband Hades. Both appealed to Zeus for a solution to this problem. Zeus pleased both by saying that Persephone would spend half of her time in the Underworld with Hades and the other half on Olympus with her mother. In this way, we are told, winter comes when Persephone goes down to the Underworld to be with her husband. Then later, when it is time for her to return to Olympus, the winter cloak of death melts and there is a rebirth of life over the land.

The Hindus looked on Virgo as *Kauni*, or "the Maiden." Others have seen her as the Woman in a Ship holding a stalk of wheat in her hand. The

The "Sombrero" Galaxy (M 104, or NGC 4594) in Virgo, as seen edge-on through the 200-inch telescope. See con- stellation diagram and spring star chart for location. HALE OBSERVATORIES.

Persians called her *Khosha,* or "the Ear of Wheat." The Arabs called her the Innocent Maiden, but since it was against their religion to draw pictures of human forms, they showed the constellation simply as a sheaf of wheat. The Hebrews called her *Bethulah,* meaning "Abundance in Harvest." The more we were to add to this list, the more we would find our fair Virgo watching over our wheat, carrots, and string beans.

The stars forming Virgo really don't suggest a human form, or a sheaf of wheat for that matter. So you might do better in this instance for settling for a geometric shape that you find easy to remember.

As you become familiar with this constellation, spend some time searching the area marked on the chart. Within this lopsided square is a treasure chest of sky objects the ancients could never have dreamed of. Binoculars will bring this area alive with interesting objects. By this time in your observing you probably have seen several star clusters and are now familiar with these splendid objects. In Virgo you will be treated to the sight of a cluster of galaxies. And more such galactic clusters await you in the region of the little constellation above Virgo, the one called Coma Berenices, or Berenice's Hair. In the Virgo cluster alone are thousands of galaxies. Also try to locate M 87. This is not a star cluster, but a spherical galaxy. And try to find M 104, the so-called Sombrero Galaxy, a spiral galaxy located just to the right of the star Spica.

The brightest star in Virgo is the brilliant white star Spica (magnitude of 0.9). It was by observing Spica (and the star Regulus) that the famous Greek astronomer Hipparchos (see page 178) discovered that the Spring and Autumn Equinoxes do not have fixed positions, but that they creep along the Zodiac over periods of thousands of years. However, it seems that the Egyptians, much earlier, were aware of this motion since they had observed that the star Thuban (in Draco) was not always the Pole Star.

The second brightest star in Virgo is the bright yellow one once called Vindemiatrix (mag. 2.8). The pale yellow star called Zavijava (mag. 3.9), from the Arabic *Al Zawiah,* meaning "the Corner," refers to the part of this constellation that was known at one time as the Kennel (for the two dogs, of course).

The best time to observe Virgo is from April through June.

COMA BERENICES *(Berenice's Hair)* ☆☆☆☆☆☆☆☆☆☆

We just mentioned this small constellation located above Virgo and to the right of Boötes as being a rich area of the sky in which to find galaxies beyond our own. This little group of faint stars did not gain an official place among the other constellations until fairly recent times. But many names had been given to it over the centuries. The ancient Chinese alone called it by more than a half dozen names. The ancient Egyptians seem to have called it simply Many Stars. One story has it that an Egyptian queen of the third century B.C., named Berenice, was grief-stricken when her husband went off to war. So concerned was she for his safe return that she promised the gods that she would cut off her beautiful hair if he returned safely.

In due course he did return, and faithful to her word she cut off her hair and placed it in the temple as an offering to the gods who had watched over her husband.

Now it happened that on one night when there was no Moon and the land was all darkness, Berenice's husband longed to see his wife's beautiful hair again and visited the temple. He was met by

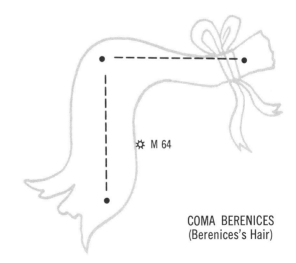

COMA BERENICES
(Berenices's Hair)

This Galaxy (M 64, or NGC 4725) in Coma Berenices) was photographed without its supernova May 10, 1940 (top), then with the supernova January 2, 1941. HALE OBSERVATORIES.

the temple guardians who told him that only moments ago the hair had disappeared, an act of the gods. So pleased were the gods with Berenice's sacrifice that they placed her hair in the sky for all to admire. Thereafter, all the King had to do to see his wife's hair was look up to the sky.

If you manage to find the three faint stars marking this constellation, binoculars will reveal numerous fainter ones within the triangle.

The best time to observe this constellation is from April through August.

LEO *(the Lion)* ☆☆☆☆☆☆☆☆☆☆☆☆☆☆☆☆☆☆☆☆☆☆☆☆☆☆☆☆☆☆☆☆

Between Virgo on the left and Cancer on the right lies another Zodiac constellation, Leo. The Lion should leap out at you with his two easily recognized parts—a great sky sickle for his shaggy

head and a right triangle for his hindquarters and
tail. At the bottom of the sickle is the bright star
Regulus marking Leo's heart. And the bright star
Denebola marks the King of Beasts's tail.

Lions are known to be hot-weather animals and
long have had the reputation of being bold, strong,
and ruling over all other animals except man. It is
not surprising, then, to find Leo given a prominent
position among the stars. And the particular place
he occupies also should not come as a surprise to us.
For some 4,000 years ago the Sun reached its highest
point in the summer sky—Summer Solstice—amid
that group of stars we now know as Leo. It would
seem natural to associate that group of stars with
some symbol of the hot summer months—in short,
the lion, which was then a common beast in Egypt.
The fact that the Egyptians worshiped lion-gods is
further evidence of the importance this beast held
in Egyptian life. The Egyptians believed that the
world was created at a time when the Sun rose in
Leo near the star Denebola. As a lion, the constellation Leo was known as far back as Sumerian times

About 4,000 years ago the Sun reached its highest point
in the sky (Summer Solstice) when it was in the constellation Leo, the Lion. This may account for the Egyptians
worshipping lion-gods. The Egyptians further believed
that the world was created when the Sun rose in Leo near
the star Denebola. Detail from the *Rosarium Philo-
sophorum*, 1550.

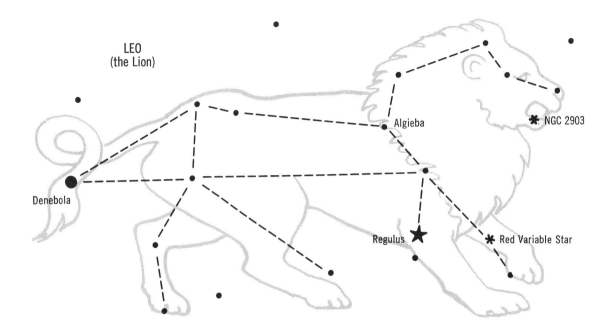

LEO
(the Lion)

NGC 2903

Algieba

Denebola

Regulus

Red Variable Star

and the constellation was passed along to the Babylonians, Greeks, Romans, and others.

We met Leo as the Nemean Lion back on page 64 in the first labor performed by Hercules. He was to kill this ferocious beast who descended to Earth from the Moon. Hera then raised the animal up to the sky and so immortalized him as a constellation. In earlier mythology of the Sumerians, Leo probably was the monster Khumbaba, who was killed by the adventurer Gilgamesh. At this time in history Leo covered a much larger area of the sky than he does now, and what is now Coma Berenices was once the fluffy tail of Leo. Around 240 B.C., however, the astronomer-priests under Ptolemy III robbed Leo of his splendid tail when they invented the new constellation, Berenice's Hair.

The famous Egyptian Sphinx, that creature with a woman's head and a lion's body, may also represent our Leo. As mentioned earlier, the constellation Leo was associated with the heat of summer when the Sun passed through Leo, after which it then entered Virgo. It may well be that since these two constellation figures were associated with the heat of summer they were combined in the form of a single creature, the Sphinx. But this is speculation only.

Again, Leo has nearly always been associated with fire, light, and the triumph of good over evil. To the Persians he was *Ser*, to the Turks, *Artan*, to the Syrians, *Aryo*, to the Jews, *Arye*, and to the Babylonians, *Aru*. All mean "Lion." As you found earlier, many of the constellations were renamed by the Church in the early days of Christianity. Leo is no

exception. It seemed natural to snatch him away from the old mythology and put him in a compound as one of Daniel's lions. To the Akkadians he was *Pa-pil-sak,* or "the Great Fire." As a symbol of strength Leo is with us today as the lion on the royal arms of England.

The brightest star in Leo is the triple and brilliant star Regulus (magnitude of 1.4). See if you can find its blue companion. Even though it is among the faintest of our first-magnitude stars, Regulus has long been considered the ruling star of the heavens, and so the Babylonians called it *Sharru*, "the King." In India it was *Magha*, "the Mighty," and in Persia it was *Miyan*, "the Center." Since Regulus marked the heart of the Lion, there is a saying more than 2,000 years old telling us that "if the star of the great lion is gloomy the heart of the people will not rejoice."

Try to find the lovely star Algieba (mags. 2.2 and 3.5), which is the third star up in the sickle from Regulus. Some say that it is the most beautiful double star seen from northern latitudes. It is yellow

A spiral galaxy (NGC 2903) in Leo, as seen through the 200-inch telescope. See constellation diagram and spring star chart for location. HALE OBSERVATORIES.

with a green companion, but you need at least a three-inch telescope to split it. See if you can spot the interesting red variable star just to the right of Regulus, which has a period of about 313 days. When dimmest you cannot see it without binoculars or a small telescope, but when brightest it is a fine naked-eye object. If you have a telescope, see if you can find NGC 2903, off the tip of the Sickle. Here is another spiral galaxy.

The second brightest star in Leo is Denebola (mag. 2.1), a blue star taking its name from the Arabic *Al Dhanab al Asad,* meaning "the Lion's Tail."

The best time to observe Leo is from February through June.

HYDRA (the Many-headed Monster) ☆☆☆☆☆☆☆☆☆☆

Hanging just under the brightest star in Cancer and a bit to the right and down from Regulus is the head of Hydra. This is the longest constellation in the sky. It stretches one-quarter of the way around the heavens. From its head it droops south and east, looping down under Virgo and continuing on a bit further with its tail pointing at Libra. On its back Hydra carries the two smaller constellations, Crater and Corvus. Aside from having one bright star, Hydra can boast of little else, although its head is formed by a neat cluster of five stars.

We met Hydra in the summer sky as the object of Hercules' second labor. He had to slay this many-headed monster, which grew two heads each time one was cut off. To find out how Hercules managed the situation, see page 64. Another story about Hydra describes him not as a dragon-monster but as a water-serpent.

One day the Sun-god Apollo sent his pet raven down to Earth to bring the thirsty god a cup of fresh spring water. Now Apollo's sacred raven was not a very dependable bird. On arriving at the spring the raven saw that a fig tree was just beginning to bear fruit.

"What matter if I wait only a few days until the fruit ripens?" the raven asked itself. And it waited. When the fruit ripened the raven then stayed

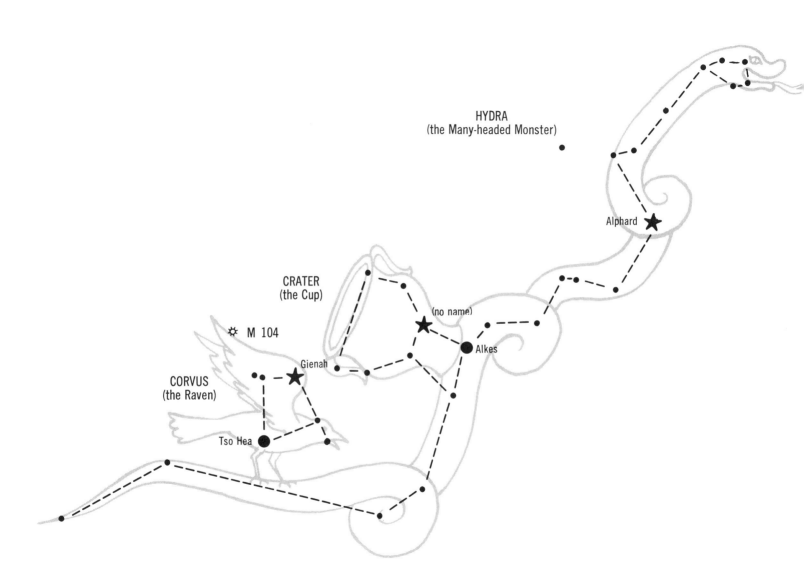

HYDRA
(the Many-headed Monster)

Alphard

CRATER
(the Cup)

(no name)

☼ M 104

Gienah

Alkes

CORVUS
(the Raven)

Tso Hea

several more days eating the fruit until it was all gone. He then filled the cup with fresh spring water but realized that his master would be angry for the long delay. Then he noticed a water-serpent nearby and grasped it in his claws. So with cup in mouth and serpent dangling from his claws, the raven flew up to Heaven. He explained to Apollo that the serpent had attacked him and that is what caused the delay.

Apollo was not taken in by the lie. And he was so angry with the bird that he flung him, cup, and serpent out of Heaven. Today we see them together in the sky as Crater, the Cup, and as Corvus, the Raven, perched on the serpent's back. This myth gave rise to two alternate names for Corvus as a constellation: *Avis Ficarius*, or "the Fig Bird," and *Emansor*, or "One Who Lingers Too Long."

As you try to trace the entire length of Hydra across the sky, remember that you cannot see it all until Crater crosses the meridian, that imaginary line crossing your overhead position and extending down the horizon at the north and south points.

Hydra has only one bright star, the orange star called Alphard (magnitude of 2.0), from the Arabic *Al Fard al Shuja*, meaning "the Solitary One in the Serpent." It is the star just southeast of Hydra's head, lying midway between the head and Crater.

Hydra is best observed from February through May.

CORVUS (the Raven) ☆☆☆☆☆☆☆☆☆☆☆☆☆☆☆☆☆☆☆☆☆☆☆

This small constellation is one member of the trio formed by Crater and Hydra (see above) and it was well known by the Greeks and Romans. According to an account differing from the one just given, Apollo fell in love with Coronis, daughter of King Phlegyas, but was so jealous that he sent his pet raven to spy on her. For his faithful services to the Sun-god, Corvus was given an honored place among the stars.

But another version of the myth has it that when Corvus returned to report to his master, Apollo was furious with what the bird had to tell him and cast him into the Underworld. At the same time he turned the raven's previously silver plumage to black, as related in these lines from the Roman poet Ovid:

> Then he turned upon the Raven,
> "Wanton blabbler! See thy fate!
> Messenger of mine no longer,
> Go to Hades with thy prate!
>
> "Weary Pluto with thy tattle!
>   Hither, monster, come not back;
> And—to match thy disposition—
>   Henceforth be thy plumage black!"

The brightest star in Corvus is seen at the upper right corner of the rectangle and is called Gienah (magnitude of 2.6), from the Arabic *Al Janah al Ghurab al Aiman*, meaning "the Right Wing of the Raven." The second brightest star in this constellation forms the lower left corner of the rectangle and has the Chinese name of *Tso Hea* (mag. 2.7), meaning "Left Hand." The ancient Chinese saw the stars in this constellation as an imperial chariot

ruling the wind. Corvus has been called the Sail by mariners.

The best time to observe Corvus is April through June.

CRATER (the Cup) ☆☆☆☆☆☆☆☆☆☆☆☆☆☆☆☆☆☆☆☆☆☆☆☆☆

This small constellation also is one member of the trio formed by Corvus and Hydra (see above). For reasons mentioned in our account of Hydra, the Greeks called this constellation the Goblet of Apollo, also the Water Bucket. In both Arabic and Persian myths the constellation was given names meaning a vessel for storing wine. This constellation, along with certain other stars of Hydra, may have formed the ancient Chinese constellation known as the Heavenly Dog. Certain of the early Christians looked on Crater as the Wine Cup of Noah.

One Greek myth accounts for this constellation without referring either to Hydra or to Corvus. It tells of the nobleman Mastusius and his daughter. Now a plague had gripped the land of King

Demophon. The king was told by an oracle that the only way to prevent all the people in the land from dying was to sacrifice a girl from a noble family once each year to the gods.

Following the oracle's advice, the king each year drew lots in order that a girl of noble birth might be selected for the sacrifice. But he did not include his own three daughters in the lottery. On learning that the king exempted his own three daughters, Mastusius said that he did not see why his daughter should be included either. The King became angry and ordered that Mastusius's daughter be sacrificed, without a drawing being held.

Now Mastusius was grief-stricken and very angry at the king but he did not show it. Instead he pretended that all was well, as before. Later, Mastusius invited the king and his daughters to a celebration on a day when he knew that the king would be late. However, King Demophon sent his daughters on ahead, which was just what Mastusius had wanted. When the girls arrived, Mastusius killed them and mixed their blood with some wine. When Demophon arrived he was served a bowl of the wine and greedily drank it. When told that he had been tricked, Demophon ordered the bowl and Mastusius thrown into the harbor. We do not know what happened to Mastusius, but the bowl was placed among the stars as a warning to all those who thought of committing evil deeds.

The brightest star in Crater is the orange star Alkes (magnitude of 4.1), and it is the only star there with a name. It forms the lower right corner of the upright rectangle. Again, don't expect to find much in this part of the sky, and you might even have trouble locating Alkes. It is quite possible that a few centuries ago the star was somewhat brighter than it is now.

Crater is best observed during April and May.

There are other constellations that we could have included in our brief survey of the sky, but they have been omitted for two reasons. First, a number of them are very dim and have very little to offer in the way of exploration with binoculars or a small telescope. Among this group are such winter constellations as Monoceros, Lynx, Pyxis, Vela, Columba, Fornax, and Puppis, and such spring constellations as Antila, Canes Venatici, and Leo Minor.

The second group that has been excluded includes most of the stars forming the south circumpolar group, few of which can be seen from the Northern Hemisphere. And this is too bad because there are several bright stars in this region of the sky, not to mention one of the most beautiful of all the constellations, the Southern Cross. But again, since these stars are not visible to us in the Northern Hemisphere there is no reason to include them here.

The Zodiac

We will never know how many lifetimes it took the stargazers of many thousands of years ago to realize that the stars could be used as a clock and a calendar. But learn they did, and long before people had learned to keep records in writing. By the time the ancient Sumerians appeared on the scene well over 3,000 years ago, they had already become highly skilled stargazers who had named numerous stars and had recognized that band of calendar constellations we call the Zodiac.

THE ZODIAC IN TIME AND SPACE ☆☆☆☆☆☆☆☆

What appears to be a bowl-shaped sky dome surrounding Earth is called the celestial sphere. There is, of course, no such bowl shape in space. The stars in our galaxy are scattered every which way, some nearer, some farther, all many light-years distant. A *light-year* is equal to about ten trillion kilometers (six trillion miles). In fact, the stars are so far away that we cannot detect their real motions of many kilometers per second in relation to each other during a human lifetime.

As the diagram here shows, if we imagined Earth's equator projected onto the celestial sphere we would produce a celestial equator. The Zodiac belt of twelve constellations circles us just as the celestial equator circles us. The only difference is that the Zodiac belt is tilted at an angle to the celestial equator. Another term that we need to know to understand the Zodiac is the *ecliptic*. The ecliptic is simply the path that the Sun traces as it appears to move around the celestial sphere. The ecliptic forms the middle line along the Zodiac highway, as shown in the diagram. Each year the Sun appears to make one complete trip around the Zodiac highway. This apparent motion is due to Earth's orbital motion around the Sun.

For many centuries, though, the stargazers of old believed that the observed motions of the Sun and planets along the ecliptic and through each of the twelve Zodiac constellations were real motions. It was not until astronomers learned that Earth does not stand motionless in space, but that it revolves around the Sun, that people learned that the Sun's

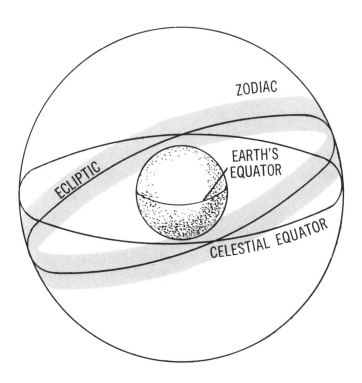

Diagram shows the relationship between the celestial equator and the ecliptic, which forms the center line of the Zodiac belt.

apparent motion around the sky is only an illusion.

Mercury, Venus, Mars, Jupiter, Saturn, and the other known planets of the Solar System also are seen to move along the ecliptic and pass through or near the twelve Zodiac constellations. This is because the planets circle the Sun along orderly orbital highways all lying in just about the same plane, except for the planet Pluto. The old Babylonians and Greeks had observed that the Moon and planets do not wander very far from the ecliptic. They stray north and south of the ecliptic by only 8°.

So we can picture the Zodiac as an imaginary circular celestial highway forming a complete circle of 360° around the sky and being 16° wide. Placed evenly along this highway are the twelve constellations in this order: Aries (the Ram), Taurus (the Bull), Gemini (the Twins), Cancer (the Crab), Leo (the Lion), Virgo (the Virgin), Libra (the Scales), Scorpio (the Scorpion), Sagittarius (the Archer), Capricorn (the Sea-Goat), Aquarius (the Water-Carrier), and Pisces (the Fishes).

As the diagram shows, the twelve constellations are spread more or less evenly along 30° intervals of the Zodiac. Centuries ago, the Sun's apparent path along the Zodiac took it through the constellation Aries, for instance, from March 21 to April 20. And the Sun was seen to enter and leave Taurus from April 21 to May 20, then enter and leave Gemini from May 21 to June 21, and so on around the Zodiac. Astrologers—those people who tell your fortune by the stars—use these old dates as if they still applied today.

The inventors of the Zodiac those several thousands of years ago made an important observation over a period of many years. They saw that at the same time each year the Sun in its apparent journey around the Zodiac crossed the celestial equator from south to north when it was in a certain part of a certain constellation. The mistake they made was supposing that this event always took place at the same time and in the same place. At the time we are talking about, the Sun happened to be seen making this famous crossing about March 21 on

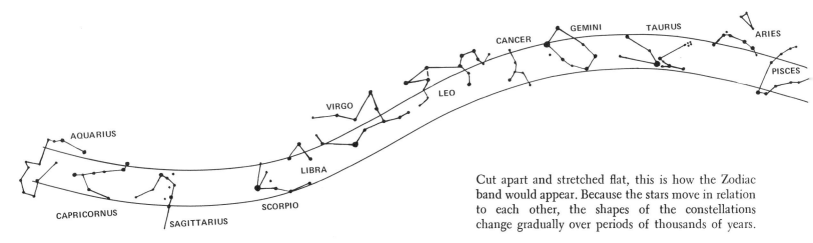

Cut apart and stretched flat, this is how the Zodiac band would appear. Because the stars move in relation to each other, the shapes of the constellations change gradually over periods of thousands of years.

our calendars today. And we call that date the Vernal (Spring) Equinox. But there is also another equinox, the Autumnal (Autumn) Equinox, which comes about September 21. On this date the Sun appears to move down and cross the celestial equator from north to south as it continues its deceptive trip along the ecliptic. You can imagine these two equinox points as being on opposite points on the celestial sphere (see diagram on page 174). At each equinox there are very nearly the same number of hours of daylight and darkness, hence *equinox*, meaning "equal-night."

If you have read the earlier sections of this book before reading this one, you found that the Babylonians regarded Spring Equinox as the beginning of the New Year since it brought spring and signaled the beginning of a new agricultural season. The Egyptians and others also cheered Spring Equinox, and for the same reason. Since the Sun entered Aries at this time of the year, it was natural to look on Aries as the "leader" of the twelve constellations and the hour hand that marked the beginning of the New Year. What better time to begin a year than when the entire countryside grows alive once again after the long winter? Since Aries was then looked on as the first constellation of the Zodiac, then the Sun's position in Aries, when the Sun was seen to cross the celestial equator, came to be called the First Point of Aries. And that term has survived the several thousands of years and to this day is used by astronomers and fortune-tellers alike.

The famous Greek astronomer Hipparchos, who lived around 150 B.C., upset this orderly picture of things. No, he said, Spring Equinox has not always occurred as we see it today when the Sun enters Aries, which meant that the dates for Aries—March 21 to April 20—are not fixed but change over the centuries. This important discovery meant that Spring Equinox had not always occurred in Aries, and that it would never occur in any of the Zodiac constellations for more than a certain length of time before moving on into the neighboring constellation westward on the Zodiac highway.

The ancient Egyptians also seem to have been aware of this migration of the First Point of Aries, but Hipparchos appears to have been the first to work out the mathematics of it. He said that the equinoxes move westward along the Zodiac at the rate of about 2° of arc every 150 years. For those of you who like dates pinned down, Spring Equinox did actually occur in Aries at the time of Hipparchos, and it had occurred there since the year 1953 B.C. But by A.D. 220, which is 2,173 years later, Spring Equinox was no longer occurring in Aries. It was occurring in the neighboring constellation of Pisces, where it occurs today.

So the First Point of Aries—that is, Spring Equinox, crept its way along the ecliptic at a predictable rate. If you had lived in the year A.D. 220, and had been born on April 12, say, you would not have been born under the sign of Aries, as the astrologers tell you to this day. Instead, you would have been born under the sign of Pisces. But from the point of view of these fortune-tellers the dates for Aries will forever be from March 21 to April 20, regardless of how the stars actually move.

Again, the equinoxes gradually creep westward around the Zodiac. And that is the important fact that Hipparchos discovered. Although Spring Equinox now occurs in Pisces, it will not remain there very much longer. In a little more than 390 years from now (about the year A.D. 2375), Spring Equinox will have wandered out of Pisces and entered the neighboring Zodiac constellation of Aquarius. Hence the "importance" of the AGE OF AQUARIUS, which is such a popular cry these days. But ask some of your astrologically-minded friends the significance of the "Age of Aquarius" and see if they know. Chances are they won't have a clue.

PRECESSION OF THE EQUINOXES ☆☆☆☆☆☆☆☆

The gradual apparent motion of the equinoxes around the Zodiac is called the *precession of the equinoxes*. Its cause remained a mystery until about 1687. At that time the famous British physicist,

Isaac Newton, framed his law of gravitation. Today it is a simple matter to understand why the equinoxes precess, or creep around the Zodiac.

Earth is not a perfect sphere. It rotates, and because it does it has developed a slight bulge at its equator. The diameter across the equator of our planet is some 42 kilometers (26.3 miles) more than the diameter from North Pole to South Pole. Also, it happens that Earth is tilted over at an angle of 23.5° in relation to the plane formed by the Sun's equator. Because of this lopsided arrangement, the Sun's and Moon's gravitational tugs on Earth are forever twisting our planet this way and that. The result is that Earth's axis gets twisted around in a circle over a certain number of years. It turns out that one complete circle takes 25,800 years. As you found earlier, this means that the North Star, presently Polaris, is not always the same star (see page 28). Another interesting effect of precession is that the Sun passes through the constellation Ophiuchus (see page 78), which is not a member of the Zodiac at all. Now this would have bothered

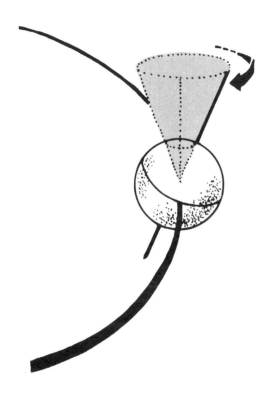

Because Earth wobbles on its axis—a motion called precession—there is a gradual change in the pattern of apparent motions of all the sky objects visible to us.

the stargazers of old. The Sun now enters Ophiuchus in early December because precession brings the ecliptic across that part of the sky at that time. The Sun actually spends more time in Ophiuchus than it does in the neighboring Zodiac constellations of Scorpius and Sagittarius.

There, then, is the "magical" Zodiac stripped of its secrets. It is nothing more than a circular belt of twelve (agreed on) constellations through which the Sun appears to pass, but doesn't, in the course of a year. The Zodiac is, of course, much more than that. To reduce it to a purely imaginary geometric form in the sky is to deny the important role it has played in the history of the human race. Even though the Zodiac has no reality in fact, its imaginary Crab, Fishes, Ram, Archer, Scorpion, Lion, and other members of the celestial zoo have influenced the lives of more people than any storyteller could possibly relate.

As Bachelard tells us on page vii, "all these constellations are beautifully false." One reason they are false is that in time they will take on new forms

About 50,000 years ago

Today

About 50,000 years from now

as viewed from Earth. We must remember that they have been changing their shapes ever so gradually ever since time began. So, good-bye, Virgo. Good-bye, Orion, So long, Sagittarius, but not for a long while as measured by Earth-time. Many more generations of Earthlings will live to gaze on these phantoms of the night sky and relive the stories they have to tell. But surely there will come a time in the life span of our species when the old myths will be cast aside and we will look at the sky realistically instead of through the eyes of the old superstitious soothsayers. Or will we?

Because the Universe is such a large and complex place, it seems unlikely that people will ever come to know it completely. Surely we will come to know parts of it very well, as we do today. But, for every part we come to know, two new and mysterious

Because the stars are in motion in relation to each other, the constellations are ever changing their shapes. The Big Dipper appears to be changing as shown here.

parts will be revealed, just as the many-headed Hydra grew two new heads each time one was lopped off.

How does man maintain his sanity in a Universe that becomes ever more complex and appears to be unknowable? According to the French philosopher Henri Bergson, human intelligence came equipped with a kind of safety valve, which is superstition. Bergson described superstition as "the ability of intelligence to shut itself off in time of stress and to accept a counterfeit experience in the place of a real one." In short, myths. When unable to understand a mysterious part of the Universe with the rational mind, invent a myth. An illiterate nomad crossing the broad Sahara by night, and an astronomer in his observatory, may both be gazing at the same object in the heavens and asking essentially the same question about it. But the answer each eventually comes up with is produced by different parts of our human intelligence. While the nomad may rely on counterfeit experience and invent a myth, the scientist draws on real experience and invents a hypothesis. Each, in his own way, has succeeded in making the Universe a knowable and orderly place again, for a while at least, but how different are the routes along which their minds travel, and how different the quality and usefulness of the knowledge each succeeds in acquiring.

Greek and Roman Gods and Goddesses

God's Function	Greek Name	Roman Name
King of Gods	Zeus	Jupiter
God of the Sea	Poseidon	Neptune
God of the Underworld	Hades	Pluto
Messenger of the Gods	Hermes	Mercury
God of War	Ares	Mars
The God's Smith	Hephaestus	Vulcan
God of Light (and the Sun)	Helios	Apollo
Goddess of Wild Animals (and the Moon)	Artemis	Diana
Goddess of Wisdom	Athene	Minerva
Queen of Heaven	Hera	Juno
Goddess of Agriculture	Demeter	Ceres
Goddess of the Hearth	Hestia	Vesta
Goddess of Love	Aphrodite	Venus
God of Wine	Dionysos	Bacchus
God of Love	Eros	Cupid
God of Time	Chronos	Saturn
Queen of the Underworld	Persephone	Proserpina

Watching Meteor Showers

Now that you are able to locate many constellations and can find your way around the sky, you will be able to enjoy the meteor showers that occur during several months of the year. A *meteor* is the streak of light resulting from the frictional burning of a lump of stone or metal, called a *meteoroid*, as it passes through Earth's atmosphere. If the meteoroid survives the journey and strikes the ground it is known as a *meteorite*.

You do not need any special equipment to observe meteor showers. The best time to look is after midnight, because at that time Earth's rotation is carrying you toward the meteors. Between sunset and midnight Earth's rotation is carrying you away from the meteors so you can expect to see fewer during this time.

In addition to the single, or *sporadic*, meteors that you can see nearly any night, at certain times of the year showers of meteors appear to be "raining" out of certain constellations. Those meteor swarms that rain out of Leo, for example, are called Leon*ids*, those from Orion are called Orion*ids*, and so on.

Once you have located a meteor shower, try setting up a camera on a tripod and open the lens to the time exposure stop. A ten-minute exposure produces a rather impressive photograph.

Name of Shower	When It Appears	Meteor Rate per Hour
Quadrantids	Jan. 3	40
Lyrids	Apr. 20-22	15
Aquarids	May 5	20
Aquarids	July 29	20
Perseids	Aug. 12	50
Orionids	Oct. 15-25	25
Taurids	Oct. 26-Nov. 16	15
Leonids	Nov. 15-20	15
Geminids	Dec. 9-13	50
Ursids	Dec. 21-22	15

Note that these dates are not necessarily exact, so begin looking a few days early and keep looking a few days late. The Quadrantids, Perseids, and Geminids tend to be fairly reliable from year to

"The stars fell like flakes of snow," said one observer of the Leonid Shower of meteors, November 13, 1833. Another observer, also believing that meteors were falling stars, thought that there would be no stars left in the sky the next night. THE AMERICAN MUSEUM-HAYDEN PLANETARIUM.

year, both in their times of appearance and the number of meteors per hour. The Leonids, on the other hand, are quite unreliable. Sometimes they put on a spectacular show while at other times you may fail to see much action at all.

During the famed November, 1833, Leonids shower, more than 200,000 meteors were visible per hour! Many people then thought that the end of the world was at hand. The Leonid shower of November, 1966, produced meteors at the rate of 100 per *second* for short periods. A meteor as bright as a first-magnitude star can be produced by a meteorite weighing as little as 1/100 of an ounce. A meteoroid about two centimeters (about an inch) across can produce a meteor as bright as the full moon. These whoppers are called *fireballs* or *bolides*.

The Brightest Stars

Star	Constellation	Magnitude	Culmination (9:00 p.m.)	Distance (light-years)
Sirius	Canis Major	—1.47	Feb. 15	8.7
Vega	Lyra	0.04	Aug. 10	26.5
Arcturus	Boötes	—0.06	June 10	36.0
Rigel	Orion	0.14	Jan. 20	900.0
Capella	Auriga	0.05	Jan. 20	45
Procyon	Canis Minor	0.37	Mar. 1	11.3
Altair	Aquila	0.77	Sept. 1	16.5
Betelgeuse	Orion	0.41	Feb. 1	520.0
Aldebaran	Taurus	0.86	Jan. 15	68.0
Spica	Virgo	0.91	May 25	220.0
Antares	Scorpius	0.92	July 10	520.0
Pollux	Gemini	1.16	Mar. 1	35.0
Fomalhaut	Piscis Australis	1.15	Oct. 15	22.6
Deneb	Cygnus	1.26	Sept. 15	1,600.0
Regulus	Leo	1.36	Apr. 9	84.0
Castor	Gemini	1.97	Mar. 1	45.0
Elnath	Taurus	1.65	Jan. 25	300.0
Alnilam	Orion	1.70	Jan. 28	1,600.0

Glossary

ANGULAR DISTANCE The distance between two objects measured by an angle. The angular distance between two stars, for example, could be found if you project a line to Star A and another line to Star B. The angle formed at your position becomes the angular distance.

ANGULAR VELOCITY The rate at which an object moves through an angle as the object travels along a curve. For example, the tip of a clock hand moves faster than a point midway down the hand, but both the tip and the midpoint have the same angular velocity, of 6° of arc per minute.

APHELION The most distant point from the Sun a planet or comet may reach as it travels in its orbit.

APOGEE The most distant point from Earth that the Moon and satellites may reach as they travel in their orbits.

APPARENT BRIGHTNESS The measure of a star's observed brightness; how bright a star appears to the eye as opposed to its actual brightness, or luminosity. The farther away a light source is from the observer, the less its apparent brightness will be, although its luminosity does not change.

APPARENT MOTION   The motion of any celestial object as seen from Earth, which itself is moving.

ASTROLOGY   An extremely old belief that the relative positions and motions of stars and planets have a controlling influence on character, occupation, health, disposition, wealth, and quality of life in people, animals, plants, nations, and institutions such as IBM and The International Red Cross. The science of astronomy grew out of astrology more than 2,000 years ago.

ASTRONOMY   The science dealing with celestial bodies, their distances, luminosities, sizes, motions, relative positions, composition, and structure. The word comes from the Greek and means "the arrangement of the stars."

AUTUMNAL EQUINOX   About September 21, at which time the Sun crosses the celestial equator from north to south. On Autumnal Equinox the hours of sunlight and darkness are nearly the same everywhere on Earth, but afterward the days begin to get shorter in the Northern Hemisphere. Autumnal Equinox, then, is one of the two points where the ecliptic crosses the celestial equator. (For the other point, see VERNAL EQUINOX.)

BLUE GIANT   An especially massive, large, and luminous star, such as Mirfak and Rigel, which are seen to shine with a bluish-white light. The core temperatures and surface temperatures of these short-lived stars are many times higher than those of less massive stars such as the Sun.

CANCER, TROPIC OF   The northernmost latitude at which the Sun appears directly overhead—23½° North Latitude.

CELESTIAL EQUATOR   The equator on the celestial sphere; more properly, the circle formed where the plane of Earth's equator is projected onto the celestial sphere.

CELESTIAL SPHERE   The stars and planets appear to move along the inner surface of a great hollow globe, one hemisphere of which you see as you observe the stars. Earth lies at the center of this so-called celestial sphere.

CELESTIAL POLES   On the celestial sphere, those points which correspond to Earth's North and South Poles. Picture them as extensions of Earth's axis.

CIRCUMPOLAR STARS   Stars that never set. They remain visible above the horizon throughout the night and throughout the year.

CLUSTERS   1. *Globular*—clusters of a great number of stars packed relatively closely together in space and spherical in shape. They surround our own galaxy and exist in the Andromeda galaxy. 2. *Open* (or *Galactic*)—a star group with no particular shape but which moves through our galaxy; the Pleiades, for example.

CONSTELLATION   The grouping of certain stars into imaginary figures on the celestial sphere. The ancients recognized the groups as human and animal figures; for example, Orion "the Hunter" and so on. By international agreement, astronomers recognize a total of 88 constellations.

CULMINATION   When a celestial body reaches its highest point in the sky and crosses the observer's celestial meridian.

DOUBLE STARS   Two stars held in gravitational association with each other and revolving around a common center of mass. Also called "binary" stars. Some star systems, such as the one to which Alpha Centauri belongs, have three or more stars held in gravitational association, and are known as multiple star systems.

ECLIPSE   The partial or total blocking from view of one celestial object by another passing in front of it. A lunar eclipse occurs when the Moon passes through Earth's shadow. Solar eclipses: 1. Partial—the Moon blocks only part of the Sun from view. 2. Total—the Moon completely covers the Sun's disk. 3. Annular—the Moon covers all the Sun's disk except a narrow outer rim. This happens because when the Moon is at its greatest distance from Earth it does not appear quite as large as the Sun's disk.

ECLIPSING DOUBLE STARS   When the two stars in a double-star system are situated in such a way that one is sometimes hidden behind the other. At such times of alignment the double star appears dimmer than when part or all of the second star is also visible.

ECLIPTIC   The path the Sun and planets appear to travel around the sky in one year. It forms a great circle on the celestial sphere.

EQUINOXES   The two days of the year when the hours of sunlight and darkness are very nearly the same all over Earth. This occurs around March 21 (Vernal Equinox) and September 21 (Autumnal Equinox).

FIRST POINT OF ARIES   That point where the Sun crosses the celestial equator at Vernal Equinox.

Although Vernal Equinox occurred in Aries many centuries ago, it now occurs in the constellation Pisces.

GALAXY   A vast collection of stars, gas, and dust held together gravitationally. Spiral galaxies are very bright and have a dense nucleus of stars with less dense spiral arms. Our galaxy, the Milky Way, is a spiral galaxy, as is the Andromeda Galaxy. Barred spiral galaxies have arms extending outward from the ends of a central bar. Elliptical galaxies are slightly flattened, sphere-shaped galaxies. Irregular galaxies have no regular shape. The neighboring galaxies, called the Clouds of Magellan, are both irregular galaxies.

GLOBULAR CLUSTER   A collection of about 100,000 or more stars forming a globular shape. A halo of about 100 globular clusters form a sphere around the central part of our galaxy.

LIGHT-YEAR   The distance that light travels in one year, at the rate of 299,800 kilometers (185,900 miles) per second, which comes to about 10 trillion kilometers (6 trillion miles).

MAGNITUDE   Apparent, or visual, magnitude is a convenient way to talk about the relative visual brightness of the stars as we see them in the sky. The higher the magnitude number of a star, the fainter the star appears to us. Some of the nearby brightest stars have a magnitude of 1, and are said to be 1st magnitude stars. Stars that appear two-and-a-half times dimmer than 1st magnitude stars have a visual magnitude of 2, and stars appearing two-and-a-half times dimmer than 2nd magnitude stars have a visual magnitude of 3, and so on. The very brightest-appearing sky objects are given negative magnitudes. For example, the Sun has a visual magnitude of -27, the Moon, -10, and a bright comet, about -5. The faintest stars visible to the unaided eye are magnitude 6.

MERIDIAN   A line of longitude on Earth's sphere, or a similar line on the celestial sphere; a line from north to south points on the horizon passing through the zenith.

MULTIPLE STARS   Many stars appear as a single star when viewed only by the unaided eye. When seen through a telescope, however, they are shown to be made up of two or more stars. Castor, for example, is made up of six stars.

NEBULA   A great cloud of dust and gas within a galaxy. Some nebulae, said to be reflection nebulae, reflect light generated by nearby stars, or by stars embedded within the nebula. Other nebulae are dark and so are called dark nebulae. Still others reradiate energy emitted by stars embedded in the nebulae and are called emission nebulae. And still others take the form of a great shell of gas cast off by an eruptive, or explosive, star. These are called planetary nebulae because they were once mistaken for planets within the Solar System.

NOVA   A star that, for some reason not yet fully understood, bursts into brilliance. Within a few days a typical nova may become hundreds of thousands of times brighter than usual, then it becomes somewhat less brilliant, and after a few months or longer the star returns to its pre-nova brightness. Certain planetary nebulae may be the result of nova eruptions. (See also SUPERNOVA.)

PARSEC   A unit of distance equal to 3.26 light-years.

PERIGEE   That point in the orbit of the Moon at which it reaches its closest possible distance to Earth; also of artificial satellites' closest approach to Earth.

PERIHELION   That point in the orbit of a planet or other member of the Solar System at which it reaches the closest possible approach to the Sun.

PERIOD   The time a variable star takes to complete one cycle of going from bright to dim and back to bright again. The periods of some variables are measured in hours, while the periods of others are measured in weeks or months. Also, the length of time it takes one celestial object to complete one orbit about another. Earth's orbital period, for example, is 365 days.

PLANET   Celestial objects that shine by reflected light from a star about which they are held gravitationally captive and about which they revolve. There are nine known primary planets in the Solar System, plus about 33 known moons, thousands of rock and metal fragments known as asteroids (in orbits lying between Mars and Jupiter), plus one known planetoid in an orbit between Saturn and Uranus.

POINTERS, THE   Two stars in the Big Dipper, Dubhe and Merak, that are aligned with and "point" to the Pole Star, Polaris.

PRECESSION   A gradual change in the direction of tilt of Earth's axis due to gravitational attraction of the Sun and Moon, which tend to pull Earth's equatorial bulge into line. This double attraction causes Earth to wobble slightly, like a spinning top. The axis completes one rotation in about 25,800 years, which means that Polaris has not always been the Pole Star, nor will it always continue to be.

RED GIANT   An enormous star that shines with a

red light because of its relatively low surface temperature (of about 3,000 K). It is now thought that most, if not all, stars go through a red giant stage after they exhaust their core hydrogen and the core collapses gravitationally. The star then swells up, becoming a red giant.

REVOLUTION The motion of one body around another. The Moon revolves about Earth; the planets revolve about the Sun.

ROTATION The motion of a body around its axis. The Sun and all the planets rotate, Earth completing one rotation about every 24 hours.

SOLSTICES The highest and lowest points from the celestial equator reached by the Sun as it appears to travel along the ecliptic. The northernmost point is called Summer Solstice (about June 22). The southernmost point is called Winter Solstice (about December 22). The Summer Solstice point lies in Gemini and the Winter Solstice point lies in Sagittarius. When at these points, the Sun appears to stand still momentarily.

STAR A hot, glowing globe of gas that emits energy. The Sun is a typical—and our closest—star. Most stars are enormous compared with planets. Stars generate energy by the fusion of atomic nuclei in their dense and hot cores. Stars seem to be formed out of dense clouds of gas and dust, evolve through various stages, and finally end their "lives" as dark, cold objects called black dwarfs.

SUPERNOVA A giant star whose brightness is tremendously increased by a catastrophic explosion. Supernova stars are many thousands of times brighter than ordinary nova stars. In a single second, a supernova releases as much energy as the Sun does over a period of about 60 years.

VARIABLE STAR A star that is not uniform in its brightness, one that becomes bright, reaching "maximum," then grows dim, reaching "minimum." The cycle repeats itself over periods of hours or years. Variable stars without proper names are given one or two letters with their constellation name following: for example, W Virginis, or RV Tauri.

Others are given the letter "V" followed by numbers and their constellation name: for example, V335 Sagitarii. 1. Pulsating Variables—These include many groups: Beta Canis Majoris Stars have short periods of only an hour or two and are not too common. Cluster Variables have periods from one-and-a-half to 24 hours and are white giants. Classical Cepheids are yellow supergiants with periods from one to 45 days and are among the brightest stars, with magnitudes smaller than -2. Type II Cepheids usually have periods of 16 to 17 days. RV Tauri Stars have periods usually less than 100 days and are less regular than the Cepheids. Long-Period Variables are the red giants or supergiants having periods between 100 days and 1,000 days. One cycle of these stars may differ considerably from the next cycle. 2. Explosive Variables—

See Nova and Supernova. 3. Irregular Variables— These include two groups of stars: Flare Stars are found among many red stars that are not giant stars. Within five minutes, these stars throw off great flares in a violent display, increasing their brightness by one magnitude. Their outbursts are not predictable. T Tauri Stars grow bright and dim without notice. They all are associated with clouds of dust and gas which they seem to be drawing into themselves. When an excessive amount of the material is drawn into the star, the star brightens. All the Irregular Variables are red giant stars.

Zodiac   The zone 16° wide stretching around the sky and centered on the ecliptic. The Moon and most of the planets revolve about the Sun in this zone, as seen from Earth.

Index

199